THE PURPOSE OF LIFE

As revealed by near-death experiences from around the world

David Sunfellow

Copyright © 2019 by David Sunfellow

All rights reserved.

David Sunfellow
P.O. Box 2242
Sedona, Arizona 86339 USA
thepurposeoflife-nde.com

Cover design by David Sunfellow
Book Layout © 2017 BookDesignTemplates.com

The Purpose of Life
As Revealed by Near-Death Experiences from Around the World
David Sunfellow
KDP ISBN – 9781797012032
Version 3.1

*To everyone
who seek answers
to life's big questions:
Who are we?
Where are we from?
What is the purpose of life?*

*For the first time in human history,
we finally have authoritative answers to these questions.
May the fantastic stories and quotes in this book
lift your spirits and light your way...*

Contents

Introduction

- *Chapters with companion videos*
- *+ New chapters added to this book*

LOVE & LIFE REVIEWS

1 - Love The Person You're With (Howard Storm) *
2 - The Golden Rule Dramatically Illustrated (Kenneth Ring) *
3 - Operation Chop-Chop (Tom Sawyer)
4 - The Full Consequences Of My Actions (Rene Jorgensen) *
5 - The Greatest Of All Actions (Reinee Pasarow) *
6 - Graham Crackers & Milk (Dianne Morrissey) *
7 - The Most Important Are Often The Least Important (Pasarow) +
8 - Watering A Tree (Mohammad Z)
9 - Plants & Animals Too (Justin U)
10 - Take Care Of The Earth, Animals, One Another (Calvert) *
11 - God's Glasses (Erica McKenzie) *
12 - Everything Is Made Of LOVE! (Mary Deioma) *

HEAVENLY HUMOR

13 - The Light Has A Fantastic Sense Of Humor (Andy Petro) *
14 - The Funniest Thought In The World (John K) +
15 - The Cable Guys (Amy Call) *

THE PURPOSE OF LIFE

16 - I Don't Want To Go Back! (Howard Storm) *
17 - You Can Do Better (Mary Jo Rapini) *
18 - Part Of You Is Choosing & Participating (Naomi)
19 - Why Am I So Depressed? (Krystal Winzer) +
20 - Bring The Light Into This World (Anne Horn) *
21 - Hold The Energy Of The Light (Ellyn Dye) *
22 - God Becoming Us (Mellen-Thomas Benedict)
23 - We Come Here To Learn About Ourselves (Ryan Rampton) *
24 - True Learning Happens In The Body (Amy Call) * +
25 - A Place To Test Ourselves Under Pressure (Jean R)
26 - The Ultimate Theme Park (Duane S)
27 - Life Is Really Exciting (Natalie Sudman) * +
28 - The Truth Is Hidden While We Are Alive (Amphianda Baskett) +
29 - It's All Good (Amy Call) *
30 - One Of God's Most Astonishing Gifts (Mary Neal) +
31 - ALL Experiences Are Essential (IANDS Experiencer #1)
32 - Our Job On Earth Is Important (Heather V)
33 - Why We Are Here (Julie Aubier) *
34 - The Sweet Spot (David Sunfellow) +

BRAVE, BOLD & BEAUTIFUL

35 - I Remembered All The Answers (Amphianda Baskett)
36 - No Wonder. No Wonder. No Wonder. (Barbara Harris Whitfield)
37 - There Is Nothing To Forgive (Anita Moorjani) *
38 - Oh Beautiful Human (Mellen-Thomas Benedict) *
39 - We Are Uniquely Special (Natalie Sudman) *

40 - Dig In, Remember, Teach Others (Natalie Sudman) +
41 - Everything Was Created For Me (Jeff Olsen)
42 - God Has A Plan For Each Of Us (Mary Neal) +
43 - Anything Is Possible (Anita Moorjani)
44 - Three Discoveries (IANDS Experiencer #2) +
45 - Give Miracles The First Chance (Mellen-Thomas Benedict)

SUPER POWERS & FUTURE SELVES

46 - Aftereffects - Kenneth Ring
47 - Aftereffects - Jeffrey Long
48 - Organic Food & Healthy Lifestyles (Linn)
49 - Everything Changed (Kenneth Ring)
50 - A Life Greatly Disrupted (Cami Renfrow)
51 - People & Animals Follow Me Home (IANDS Experiencer #3)
52 - I Knew Their Story (Ana Cecilia G)
53 - All The Side Effects (IANDS Experiencer #4)
54 - Tell Her About The Light (Louisa Peck) +
55 - I Knew Their Hearts (Jeff Olsen)
56 - One Day In Manhattan (Peter Panagore)
57 - Experiencers Will Affect The Entire World (Benedict)

PARADISE LOST

58 - The Next Part Of The Journey (Ryan Rampton) *
59 - Only A Memory (Amphianda Baskett)
60 - You Can't Keep Any Of The Toys (Alon Anava) * +
61 - I Thought I Was Going To Be A Saint (Howard Storm)
62 - Enlightenment Is A Fantasy (Barbara Harris Whitfield)

63 - Egotism Is A Huge Problem (Howard Storm) * +

64 - A Double Warning (David Sunfellow) +

65 - Experiencers Are Still Human (Kenneth Ring)

66 - Don't Pine For A Near-Death Experience (Peter Panagore) *

67 - Be Careful What You Wish For (Natalie Sudman) * +

68 - Experiencers Need To Protect Themselves (Tricia Barker) * +

69 - When Hellfire Preachers Meet A Loving God (John W. Price)

70 - Become The Story (David Sunfellow)

71 - Step-By-Step, Little-By-Little (David Sunfellow)

HELL

72 - The Most Frightening Things I Have Encountered (Long) +

73 - As In This World, So In The Next - Only More So (Williams) +

74 - The Beings Of Hell: Common Characteristics (Samuel Bercholz) +

75 - A Spiritual Wakeup Call (Barbara R. Rommer) +

76 - The Same Level Of Transformation (Jeffrey Long) +

77 - Everyone Can Have A Hellish Experience (Barbara R. Rommer) +

78 - Sorted By Vibration (Arthur Yensen)

79 - Hell & The Importance Of Kindness (Samuel Bercholz) +

80 - If You End Up In Hell (David Sunfellow) +

81 - Cry Out To God (Howard Storm) +

82 - God, Help Me! (Cathleen C) +

83 - Heaven Is A Frequency (Teri R)

ANGELS

84 - Angels, Angels Everywhere (George Ritchie)

85 - A White Glow & Glint Of Lights (Linda Stewart) +

86 - Watch This! (Tricia Barker) +
87 - It's Going To Be OK (Cecil Willy) * +
88 - We All Have Guardian Angels (Lorna Byrne) +

HEAVEN ON EARTH

89 - How To Still Storms & Walk On Water (David Sunfellow)
90 - The Future Of The World (Howard Storm) *

Universal Truths (v2.2)

Special Thanks

References, Links & Resources

Experiencers & Researchers Featured In This Book

Introduction

By David Sunfellow

Every day, all over the world, an increasing number of people are reporting near-death experiences (and related phenomena). While near-death experiences have been reported since ancient times, it is only in the last few decades that we have been able to gather large numbers of these stories and systematically study them. The information that emerges from these stories, both ancient and modern, is profound. It is also remarkably consistent, instructive, and inspiring.

This book is a collection of the best stories and quotes I have come across in 40-plus years of studying NDEs. It shines a bright light on the universal truths that are championed by NDEs and reveals, in life-changing technicolor, how to apply these truths to our everyday lives.

THE PURPOSE OF LIFE

This book was first published under the title "Love The Person You're With." All 60 chapters of that book are included in this one. 31 additional chapters have been added. The book is being published with a new cover and title to reach more people. New content has been added to explore some topics in greater depth. Other tweaks, including enhanced references, have been added to make the book easier to read, remember, and study.

Each chapter consists of a remarkable story, quote, or series of quotes. Links at the end of every chapter provide background information about the experiencer or researcher who is featured. These links also lead to source materials and information pertaining to related topics.

New chapters are marked with "+" in the Table of Contents. Chapters that include " * " in the title have companion videos. A link at the bottom of video chapters allows you to watch the original video on the book's website. Be sure to take advantage of this wonderful feature. NDE stories are often more impactful when you can listen to people sharing their stories directly.

One bit of advice: **read this book slowly and carefully.** There is so much power in these accounts that you might catch fire if you read them too fast.

Or you might miss out.

Whether you are new to the subject of near-death experiences, or have studied them for decades, reading these accounts is akin to being struck by lightning. Repeatedly. Not only do they communicate universal truths with unparalleled clarity and power, but they also make it crystal clear how to apply these truths to our daily lives, which is what I care most about.

NDE Researcher Kenneth Ring said it best:

"The true promise of the NDE is not so much what it suggests about an afterlife -- as inspiring and comforting as those glimpses are -- but what it says about how to live NOW... to learn from NDErs about how to live, or how to live better, with greater self-awareness, self-compassion, and concern for others."

THE PURPOSE OF LIFE

- 1 -

Love The Person You're With *
Near-Death Experiencer Howard Storm

When Jesus told me I had to come back to the world and I was trying to convince him not to send me back, I asked him what would I do if I came back. Before he had a chance to answer, I said, "you know I am an artist and I would like to build you a shrine. I would make this shrine so big and beautiful and bizarre that people would come from all over the world out of curiosity to see what it was about. What they would find was it would be about you. That would make them think about you. That's what I would like to do if I came back."

He said, "I would rather you didn't do that."

"WHAT?!! People have been building shrines to you forever. There are lots of shrines. Why can't I build a shrine? I would like to build a shrine."

"You spent so much of your life hiding out in the studio, avoiding people, I would prefer it if you didn't avoid people by building this big shrine... I don't really care about shrines. People like to build shrines. I understand that. It makes them feel good. It does absolutely nothing for me or for God. We don't have any use for them whatsoever. If that's what amuses you, I guess that's what you gotta do. But don't do it for me. Don't deceive yourself into thinking it's something I want or need, because I don't."

"OK, you shot down my idea. What's your idea?"

"Love the person you're with."

"OK, great, I'll do that. No problem. What do you want me to do?"

"I just told you what I want you to do: love the person you're with."

"Yeah, but after I do that, what do you really want me to do?"

"No, that is what I want you to do: love the person you're with."

I said, "Well that's simple enough, that's easy, I can do that."

"Oh really. Well, that's what I want you to do. That's enough."

And I said, "How is it enough?"

"If you do that, you will change the world."

"Oh, you want me to change the world?!"

"Exactly, that's why I put you in the world in the first place: to change the world."

"Well you know there have been a lot of people who have tried to change the world and that usually turns out pretty badly. I can think of examples like Adolph Hitler, and Joseph Stalin, and Mao Tse-tung. All of them wanted to change the world and they made it worse. If I go back and try and change the world, why isn't it possible that I could make a lot of terrible mistakes and make the world a worse place?"

"The way I want you to change the world is by loving the person you are with."

"Wait a minute, that's a contradiction. You want me to change the world but you just want me to love the person I'm with?"

"Yes, that's the plan; that's The Big Plan… If you love the person you're with, then that person will go out and love the person they're with, and they will go out and love the person they're with and it will be like a chain reaction and love will conquer the world and everyone will love one another. That's God's Big Plan."

THE PURPOSE OF LIFE

"It's not going to work."

"Why won't it work?"

"I love the person I'm with. She walks across the street and gets run over by a truck. Everyone gets angry and upset."

"Yeah, that happens. But it's really God's plan and nothing is going to stop it. It's going to happen."

"Even if you had a million people, I don't think it's going to happen."

"There are more than a million people in the plan…"

"Well, from what I know of the world, you don't have enough."

"Actually, we have all the angels in the plan. There are a lot of them. There are more angels than people in the world… There are millions of people. There are all the angels. And there's God. It's inevitable. The plan is going to happen."

"If that's your plan, I'll do it, but I just don't really see much hope for it."

"You don't know enough to see how it's going to happen."

So, my solution to everything is to love one another. And when I read the Bible and found out that that was written in the Bible as Jesus' commandment: "This is my commandment, that you love one another..." That's the program. I have tried to be part of that program... So, I personally have no big plan other than to be loving.

The only fly in the ointment was that I thought it was going to be easy, and it turns out to be the hardest thing I've ever done. It sounds so simple, but it's really difficult. It's easy for me to love my mother because she was a really nice woman; a very loving woman. It's not hard to love someone who is really good and really loving. But what do you do with someone who is difficult, or really nasty? Those are hard people to love.

And what does it mean to love someone? Sometimes to love someone means you need to incarcerate them. And that's not a lot of fun. Sometimes loving someone means you have to put as much distance between them and you as possible and tell them to never call you. And that's not a lot of fun.

Loving people sounds so simple, but it's very difficult...

THE PURPOSE OF LIFE

Watch The Companion Video
thepurposeoflife-nde.com/videos/

Learn About Near-Death Experiencer Howard Storm
thepurposeoflife-nde.com/contents/

Other People Who Encountered Jesus
encounters-with-jesus.org/encounters/

- 2 -

The Golden Rule Dramatically Illustrated *

Researcher Kenneth Ring, PhD

I think this is one of the most remarkable aspects of the near-death experience and one that is not really given the amount of attention that it should. Many people know about The Light, they know about the out-of-body experience. The thing that really is, I think, important about the near-death experience in regard to the life review phenomena is that it isn't just a life review. It's a reliving of your life... When people describe the full experience, it's every single act you have done, every single thought you have thought, every single word you have spoken -- suddenly all of this is back with you. You are running through it again and you see and you experience the effects of these acts, these thoughts, and these words on other people. Let me just give you one brief example to illustrate this.

I have a friend who when growing up was kind of a roughneck; he had a hot temper; he was always getting into scrapes. One day he was driving his truck through the suburb in the town where he lived and he almost hit a pedestrian. And he got very aggravated with the pedestrian and he was a very big physical guy -- still is -- and a fight ensued. He punched this guy out and left him unconscious on the pavement, got back into his truck, and roared off.

15 years later my friend has a near-death experience... and during the near-death experience, he has a life review. In his life review, this particular scene of the fight takes place again... And he said that, as many people do, he experienced this from a dual aspect. There was a part of him that was almost as if he were high up in a building looking out a window and seeing the fight below. But at the same time he was observing the fight like a spectator, he saw himself in the fight. Except this time, he found himself in the role of the other person. And he felt all 32 blows that he had rained on this person 15 years ago now being inflicted upon himself. He felt his teeth cracking. He felt the blood in his teeth. He felt everything that this other person must have felt at that particular time. There was a complete role reversal; an empathic life review experience.

This is the sort of thing that many people report. And when they report these kinds of experiences, they realize that in our life, we are the very people that we hurt; we are the very people that we help to feel good. We experience these actions as though done to ourselves in the life review. So when people start talking about The Golden Rule in the context of the near-death experience, The Golden Rule is not just a precept for moral conduct -- it's the way it works! And you experience this during the life review. You learn that lesson in a very forceable way as a result of going through this kind of experience. And that's why, when people have NDEs, they change as much as they do! If you can even imagine what it must be like to go through your entire life and see everything you've ever done, without judgment, but from a kind of almost omniscient point of view with regard to the effects of those actions, and you see what your actions do to other people, it's a heavy kind of lesson. It's something that stays with you, and informs your conduct for the time after your near-death experience.

So it does give us a lot to think about, and that's why I say in my book "Lessons from The Light," the near-death experience isn't given just to those who have the experience, it's given to all of us to learn from, because all of us can profit from the lessons near-death experiencers learn in the course of a life review or other aspects of their experience. We can grow from these lessons. We can apply these lessons into our daily lives.

Watch The Companion Video
thepurposeoflife-nde.com/videos/

Learn About Researcher Kenneth Ring
thepurposeoflife-nde.com/contents/

THE PURPOSE OF LIFE

— 3 —

Operation Chop-Chop
Near-Death Experiencer Tom Sawyer

When I was around eight years old, my father told me to mow the lawn and cut the weeds in the yard. We had a cottage in the back and a double house in the front. Aunt Gay, my mother's sister, lived in the cottage out back. Aunt Gay was a very delightful person; she was a friend of mine as well as my aunt... She was always fun to be with. All the kids thought she was a cool person to know. She had described to me her plans for some wild flowers that grew on little vines in the backyard. "Leave them alone now, Tom," she said, "and as soon as they blossom we'll make tiaras for all the girls, and flower necklaces for some of the guys." Then everybody could pitch in, and she'd teach them how to weave such things. That was typical of her. We were looking forward to that.

However, my father told me to mow the lawn and cut the weeds.

Now, I had several choices. I could explain to my father that Aunt Gay wanted the weeds left to grow in this particular area. If he said to cut them all, I could have explained to Aunt Gay that father had just told me to mow the lawn and to cut that patch of weeds. I could ask if she wanted to make her request to my father. Or, I could methodically and deliberately go ahead and mow the yard and cut the weeds. I did that. Well, worse than that, I even came up with a name for the job. I called it "Operation Chop-Chop." I deliberately decided to be bad, to be malicious. And I went ahead, feeling the authority that my father gave me when he told me to cut the grass and the weeds.

I thought, "Wow, I got away with it; I did it. And if Aunt Gay ever says anything, I'll just tell her father told me to do it. Or if father asks me, I'll say well that's what you told me to do." And I would be vindicated. It would be okay; it would be a perfect Operation Chop-Chop. End of story. My Aunt Gay never said a word to me; nothing was ever mentioned; I got away with it totally.

Guess what? I not only relived it in my life review, but I relived every exact thought and attitude; even the air temperature and things that I couldn't have possibly measured when I was eight years old. For example, I wasn't aware of how many mosquitoes were in the area. In the life review, I could have counted the mosquitoes. Everything was more accurate than could possibly be perceived in the original event.

I not only re-experienced my eight-year-old attitude and the kind of excitement and joy of getting away with something, but I was also observing this entire event as a thirty-three-year-old adult; with the wisdom and philosophy I was able to attain by that time. But it was more than that.

I also experienced it exactly as though I was Aunt Gay, several days after the weeds had been cut, when she walked out the back door. I knew the series of thoughts that bounced back and forth in her mind.

"Oh my goodness, what has happened? Oh well, he must have forgotten. But he couldn't have forgotten, everyone was looking forward to -- Oh no, knock it off. Tommy is... He's never done anything like that. I love him so. Oh, come on, cut it out. Gee, it was so important. He had to know ... he couldn't have known."

Back and forth, back and forth, between thinking of the possibility, and saying to herself:

"Well, it is possible. No, Tommy isn't like that. It doesn't matter anyway, I love him. I'll never mention it. God forbid, if he did forget and I remind him, that will hurt his feelings. But I think that he did, though. Should I confront him with it and just ask him?"

Thought-pattern after thought-pattern. What I'm telling you is, I was in my Aunt Gay's body, I was in her eyes, I was in her emotions, I was in her unanswered questions. I experienced the disappointment, the humiliation. It was very devastating to me. It changed my attitude as I experienced it.

I experienced things that cannot be perceived. I watched me mowing the law from straight above, anywhere from several hundred to a couple of thousand feet, as though I were a camera. I watched all of that. I was able to perceive and feel and know everything about my Aunt Gay regarding our relationship in that general time frame and regarding Operation Chop-Chop.

In addition, and what is probably more important, spiritually speaking, I was able to observe the scene, absolutely, positively, unconditionally. In other words, not with the horrendous emotional ill-feelings that my Aunt Gay experienced not knowing for sure, and yet being afraid to question for fear that she would inflict some kind of dis-ease, or ill feelings on my part. God forbid, if I did it by accident and her reminder would hurt my feelings. And yet she experienced hurt in losing the flowering weeds, not being able to do the things for all the children she had promised, and constantly questioning whether I could have done it on purpose. I did experience that in this unconditional way, with this unconditional love that is only God's eyes, or the eyes of Jesus Christ, or the light of Jesus, or the light of Buddha enlightened, the spiritual entity.

It is that combination that is God unconditionally, not "Boy, Tom, you sure did a good rip-off," or "There, Tom, now do you feel bad enough?" or, "You sure were bad."

None of that, only as in the eyes of God, simple, pure, scientific observation, complete, totally, non-attachment. No judgmental aspect whatsoever. This is simultaneous with the total devastation I created in my aunt's life. And the arrogance, the snide little thoughts, the bad feelings, and the excitement of what I created in my own life at that young age, that was one event.

I wish that I could tell you how it really felt and what the life review is like, but I'll never be able to do it accurately. I'm hoping to give you just a slight inkling of what is available to each and every one of you. Will you be totally devastated by the crap you've brought into other people's lives? Or will you be equally enlightened and uplifted by the love and joy that you have shared in other people's lives?

Well, guess what? It pretty much averages itself out. You will be responsible for yourself, judging and reliving what you have done to everything and everybody in very far-reaching ways. Very small, seemingly inconsequential things such as the day when I, nine years old, walked through Seneca Park and loved the appearance of a tree. In my life review I could experience a bit of what the tree experienced in my loving it, two little photons of love and adoration. It was somewhat like the leaves acknowledging my presence. Can a tree experience that? Yes, it can. Don't go kicking trees anymore!

You do have that effect on plants. You do have an effect on animals. You do have an effect on the universe. And in your life review you'll be the universe and experience yourself in what you call your lifetime and how it affects the universe. In your life review you'll be yourself absolutely, in every aspect of time, in every event, in the over-all scheme of things in your lifetime. Your life.

The little bugs on your eyelids that some of you don't even know exist. That's an interrelationship -- you with yourself, and these little entities that are living and surviving on your eyelids. When you waved a loving goodbye to a good friend the other day, did you affect the clouds up above? Did you actually affect them? Do a butterfly's wings in China affect the weather here? You better believe they do. You can learn all of that in a life review!

As this takes place, you have total knowledge. You have the ability to be a psychologist, a psychiatrist, a psychoanalyst, and much more. You are your own spiritual teacher, maybe for the first and only time in your life. You are simultaneously the student and the teacher.

My life review was part of this experience also. It was absolutely, positively, everything basically from the first breath of life right through the accident. It was everything.

During this life review I experienced what I can only describe as "in the eyes of Jesus Christ." Meaning, I watched and observed this entire event as if I were in the eyes of Jesus Christ. Which means unconditionally.

It does not mean, "Gee, Tom, by being Christ-like, you don't hit people, you love people."

No to that. Nor was it, "Wow, God has really made you a very good specimen and your reflexes are superior. You did an excellent job in beating that man up."

No to that either. It's not judgmental or negative. I can't describe it other than with the unconditional love of Christ, the Christ who has absolute unconditional love. You will have the experience of observing something without any emotion or righteousness, or judgmental attachments. You will be able to observe history only as history, without the emotional attachments to the facts and figures. I want to also say that there were experiences of absolute love and joy...

Learn About Near-Death Experiencer Tom Sawyer
thepurposeoflife-nde.com/contents/

THE PURPOSE OF LIFE

— 4 —

The Full Consequences Of My Actions *
Near-Death-Like Experiencer Rene Jorgensen

The life review continued all the way down to third grade where there was a moment that I had totally forgotten -- I'm 27 at this point and this was in third grade... It was an instant during a break in school. I was teasing a smaller girl... I'm now seeing this event play out in front of me and I'm seeing her standing against the wall and I'm going like "na nan nan nan na na" -- teasing her and calling her names... And she's standing against the wall crying... And now I'm on the receiving end, meaning I'm her! And I'm feeling... the pain of my hurtful actions on her; I'm feeling how it feels for her to receive my actions that are very hurtful. And not only am I feeling her sorrow and her pain, but I am also sensing and understanding how my actions are impacting her future life. I'm now seeing, sensing, and feeling that she will become much more shy and introverted for the rest of her life because of my actions. But not only do I sense and feel that, I also feel the pain and sorrow in her parents because she's now going to turn out as a more shy and inward

THE PURPOSE OF LIFE

person. So I'm really feeling the full consequences -- not just that my actions are changing the life of this little girl, but I am also feeling... how my actions caused ripples far away, not just in her life, but in her parents' lives, in her whole family, also in everyone around her. So I really get a full spectrum of the full consequences -- all the links in the chain -- to... spending a few minutes in a schoolyard teasing a girl.

Watch The Companion Video
thepurposeoflife-nde.com/videos/

Learn About Near-Death-Like Experiencer Rene Jorgensen
thepurposeoflife-nde.com/contents/

- 5 -

The Greatest Of All Actions *
Near-Death Experiencer Reinee Pasarow

This recounting for the deeds of one's life is not what you would think at all in terms of this life. Because what was important were the choices I made. And what was more important than the choices I made, were my motivations and my intent, and really the state of my heart in doing any single action...

I experienced in a holographic awareness that was instantaneous how every action that one takes is like a stone cast in the water. And if it's loving, that stone... goes out and touches the first person that it's intended for and then it touches another person and then it touches another person because that person interacts with other people. And so on and so on. Every action has a reverberating effect on every single one of us on the face of this planet. So if I had committed a loving action, it was like love upon love upon love. A purely loving action was the most wonderful thing that I could ever have achieved in my life. This had more meaning than to have been a Rockefeller, or president of the United States, or to have been a great scientist, and to have invented something incredible. If I had committed a truly pure and loving action, it reverberated throughout the stuff of every individual on the planet and I felt that action reverberating through them and through myself. And I felt this in a way that is beyond what we can feel on this plane of existence.

So the significance of one's actions totally changed. What was not important was anything that I had owned or known intellectually (there is a sense of intellectual pride -- not that knowledge is bad, knowledge is good), but what was important was the purity and motivation of every action.

The most important of my actions was an instant I would never have recalled except for the near-death experience. Many years ago I had worked every summer as a volunteer with retarded children. There was a day camp that went on and I spend all summer going every day, eight hours a day, to this day camp. And there was a child, one time... I had taken a child aside on a very hot day. And this was not a charming or a particularly lovable child. But I wanted this child to feel loved; I wanted this child to feel, really, the love of God that brought him into existence and that brought us all into existence. I took him aside, although I wasn't religiously motivated, formally; I just wanted him to feel love. I took him aside and gave him something to drink and just spent some time with him. And he was very agitated, but I just wanted him to feel that love. And that was the greatest of all actions. That filled with me with unspeakable and incomprehensible joy. And it was not an action that anyone noticed. And it was not an action that I even recalled. And it was not an action that I had done with any thought of reward. It was simply an action motivated by love. By selfless love. And this had great meaning...

Watch The Companion Video
thepurposeoflife-nde.com/videos/

Learn About Near-Death Experiencer Reinee Pasarow
thepurposeoflife-nde.com/contents/

Graham Crackers & Milk *

Near-Death Experiencer Dianne Morrissey

First Excerpt:

I was always really fortunate. I came from a wonderful home, had a wonderful childhood. My parents loved me desperately. And their love compared to this woman -- you can't even compare it. When she came, she stood next to me and she extended her hand outward and said, "look there." And when I turned my head... I watched every second of my life from the moment I was born until the moment I died. And it wasn't just seeing it. I lived it again exactly the way I felt it the first time but with a new sense of intellectual understanding about how I could have done it different, what might have been better. And other things that I cared little about, that I didn't think made an impression on anybody's life at all were very significant. Probably the most important was when I worked at a convalescent hospital in high school after school and I used to give a lady graham crackers and milk before I'd leave the shift. I had no idea how much I had changed her life, how grateful, how appreciative she was. I thought it was so insignificant at that time in the 11th grade, but it wasn't. It was like every spirit looking down and saying, "Thank you for doing this. This woman had nobody. No one loved her."

Second Excerpt:

Then, my angel showed me a second vision, a scene I'd forgotten. I now saw myself at 17, when I'd worked at a convalescent hospital after school. I had grown fond of a toothless old woman who was no longer able to speak clearly, and who never had visitors. She liked to suck on graham crackers before going to bed, but no one wanted to serve her because when she had finished, she would drool as she kissed the entire length of the arm of the person feeding her. While others avoided her, I willingly fed her the cookies she adored, seeing how happy this made her.

When that scene was replayed for me, I felt as if every loving spirit in God's kingdom was thanking me in unison. I was amazed that such an act could have meant so much to God -- and to me. I felt humbled and very honored.

AS REVEALED BY NEAR-DEATH EXPERIENCES

Watch The Companion Video
thepurposeoflife-nde.com/videos/

Learn About Near-Death Experiencer Dianne Morrissey
thepurposeoflife-nde.com/contents/

THE PURPOSE OF LIFE

- 7 -

The Most Important Are Often The Least Important

Near-Death Experiencer Reinee Pasarow

From the book Answers from Heaven

First Excerpt:

In this other realm, my uncle and I were suddenly merged together... I became aware of things that I could not have known about my uncle in this world. I discovered that he was a person of tremendous courage, though to look at him in this life, you might not know it. Although he was a tall, impressive, stoic-looking individual with classic Native American features, he was also a quiet, reserved, and very humble man. During this reunion, I learned that he was someone who would stand up for things that he truly believed in and that he had struggled with and had overcome some huge challenges in his life. I had never heard him spoken of as a heroic type; however, I learned through this encounter that this courage was almost unspeakably great in him.

THE PURPOSE OF LIFE

Second Excerpt:

I came to realize that the people who were most important were often the ones who we might consider to be the least important in this world. I learned to see people very differently, in a new light. To give one example: consider someone who has fought hard to overcome addiction. Such a person might not be looked upon favorably in this physical world for having had an addiction. However, the tremendous struggle, the strength, and the courage that it took to overcome the powerful hold of addiction, is viewed as quite admirable in the next world. Here, we often judge people negatively for the challenges which they face, rather than by the character, fortitude, and courage they develop from facing and overcoming those immense challenges.

Answers from Heaven
thepurposeoflife-nde.com/books/

Learn About Near-Death Experiencer Reinee Pasarow
thepurposeoflife-nde.com/contents/

Watering A Tree

Near-Death Experiencer Mohammad Z

One example of my life review was when I was a little kid. We were traveling by car and stopped somewhere along the way. There was a river not far from the road and I was asked to go and bring some water in a bucket from that river. I went to fill up the bucket but on my way back, I felt that the bucket was way too heavy for me. I decided to empty some of the water to make the bucket lighter. Instead of emptying the water right there, I noticed a tree that was alone by itself in a dry patch of land. I took the effort to go out of my way to that tree and emptied some of the water at the tree base. I even waited there a few seconds to make sure the water is soaked in the soil and is absorbed. In my life review, I received such an applaud and joy for this simple act that it is unbelievable. It was like all the spirits in the universe were filled with joy from this simple act and were telling me, "We are proud of you." That simple act seemed to be one of the best things I had ever done in my life! This was strange to me, because I didn't think this little act was a big deal and thought I had done much more important and bigger things. However, it was shown to me that what I had done was extremely valuable because I had done it purely from the heart, with absolutely no expectation for my own gain.

Another example of my life review was when I was a 10 year old boy. I had bullied and mercilessly beaten another boy who was also around my age. He felt tortured and deeply hurt. In my life review, I saw that scene again. The boy was crying in physical and deep emotional pain. As he was walking in the street crying and going back home, he radiated negative energy which affected everything around him and on the path. People, and even birds, trees, and flies, received this negative energy from him, which kept propagating throughout the universe. Even rocks on the side of the street were affected by his pain. I saw that everything is alive and our way of grouping things in categories of "alive" and "not alive" is only from our limited physical point of view. In reality, everything is alive. I felt all of the pain and hurt that I had inflicted upon him inside of myself. When this boy went home to his parents, I saw the impact that seeing him in that state had on his parents. I felt the feeling and pain it created in them and how it affected their behavior from that point forward. I saw that as a result of this action, his parents would be always more worried when their son was away from home or if he was a few minutes late.

I saw that whenever I had done something good to anyone or anything, that I had done it to myself. And whenever I had hurt someone, I had done it to myself while actually doing that person a favor because they would receive some form of compensation or help from the universe as a result. This universal gift would be bigger than the damage I had caused to them...

Learn About Near-Death Experiencer Mohammad Z
thepurposeoflife-nde.com/contents/

NDEs On The Importance Of Plants, Animals & The Earth
the-formula.org/ndes-on-the-importance-of-caring-for-plants-animals-the-earth/

THE PURPOSE OF LIFE

Plants & Animals Too
Near-Death Experiencer Justin U

Many events in my life I experienced, not from how I remembered it, but from the point of view... of how people, animals, and the environment experienced it around me. I felt it as my own. The times I had made others happy, or sad, I felt it all as they did. It was very apparent that every single thought, word, and action affects everything around us and indeed the entire universe. Trees, plants, animals too. I have been a long-term vegetarian since about 18 years old and I know this was appreciated and is a good choice in life. Spiritually it seemed to show proof of respect for all life, and even seemed to balance some of the negative and wicked things I have done in my life. In the life review we judge ourselves; no one else does. The Light/God did not. But with no ego left -- and no lies -- we can't hide from what we have done and feel remorse and shame, especially in the presence of this love and light. Some of the things in life we think of as important don't seem to be so important there. But some of the insignificant things from the material human perspective are very important spiritually.

THE PURPOSE OF LIFE

Learn About Near-Death Experiencer Justin U
thepurposeoflife-nde.com/contents/

NDEs On The Importance Of Plants, Animals & The Earth
the-formula.org/ndes-on-the-importance-of-caring-for-plants-animals-the-earth/

- 10 -

Take Care Of The Earth, Animals, One Another *
Near-Death Experiencer Oliver John Calvert

I heard a voice say to me, "You have not fulfilled your purpose here."

And I said, "What was my purpose? I didn't have a clue. I truly didn't have a clue -- how to live, what life was about, what it was to be a man, what my goals or purpose could have been. So I said, "What was my purpose?"

And this voice says to me, "The same as every man. You were put on the Earth to take care of the Earth..." We, as men, are here to take care of the Earth. That's one of our responsibilities, as men. It was very personal. He said, "You're not to strip mine the Earth. You're not to pollute the Earth. You're not to destroy your home."

And I was being indicted because I was responsible. I was a litterer. I was one that didn't care about nature or the environment at all. And this was a beautiful home that God had created for me to live in and enjoy.

And He said, "Secondly, you are here for the animals. They look up to you. You are the one with the spirit. You are the one with reason, with intelligence, with the strength to change things, the ability to protect them and take care of them and do for them. They don't have that ability. And yet you destroy species after species."

And I knew that I was responsible, partly responsible. I had hunted for sport. I had no concern for animals. I never showed any compassion -- I didn't have any compassion for animals or people.

And He said, "Thirdly and most importantly, you are here for each other. And you -- this imperative, YOU -- I sent to be part of the answer. You've just been part of the problem..." And He began to try to teach me...

AS REVEALED BY NEAR-DEATH EXPERIENCES

Watch The Companion Video
thepurposeoflife-nde.com/videos/

Learn About Near-Death Experiencer Oliver John Calvert
thepurposeoflife-nde.com/contents/

NDEs On The Importance Of Plants, Animals & The Earth
the-formula.org/ndes-on-the-importance-of-caring-for-plants-animals-the-earth/

THE PURPOSE OF LIFE

God's Glasses *

Near-Death Experiencer Erica McKenzie

As soon as I chose to let go, that's when I was embraced by this incredible light in this tunnel that propelled me at an incredible force. It was so powerful, so magnificent, so loving -- I've never, ever felt this kind of love before. It is really a challenge to put into words, to describe the magnitude of the love and the embrace that I felt in this tunnel... I got to the very end of the tunnel where the light was and in that very moment I was delivered into the hands of God. And God and I stood together and God was on my right and heaven was behind us... As we're looking out in front of us at the galaxy and all the stars in front of us I hear, in my left ear, a vintage-sounding projector. It sounded like a movie was starting. As soon as I heard the projector going in my left ear, the stars all of a sudden lined up like a curtain and the curtain opened slowly, to the right. I heard "Three. Two. One. The Life Review of Erica McKenzie" on the projector screen. So it was God and I in a big movie theater in the galaxy. That's when my life review began.

THE PURPOSE OF LIFE

The life review was everything from day I was born until the day I took my last breath and died. In this life review, I was shown everything from things like losing my first tooth, graduating from high school, any kind of awards that I had won in athletics, or cheerleading, all of these things that were great accomplishments. They were really happy times. They were significant -- things that man deems as significant accomplishments.

As I am watching all these events unfold in chronological order, I'm actually reliving the event in that very moment as if it had just happened the first time. As we are observing it, I'm living it.

We finally get to the end on the day I died and the movie screen turned off. And then all of a sudden, in front me, I knew to look down... What appeared in front of me was a pair of eyeglasses. I've never worn glasses before and God said to put them on. I didn't know how I was going to put these glasses on because you have to understand that these glasses weren't a normal pair of glasses that you would find here on Earth. These glasses were the size of a vehicle. I'm thinking to myself, "how am I going to put these glasses on?"... I remember as soon as I had the thought "how am I going to do this?" it didn't even matter -- my hands were already drawing the glasses near to put them on my face. By the time I got them to my face it wasn't even a problem. They fit perfectly. And I could see. I could really see. And then God said "Now look."

And as soon as He said "now look" again I heard that vintage movie projector in my left ear: "Three. Two. One." The curtain opened again: "The Life Review of Erica McKenzie." So this was my second life review and this time I didn't see at all what I had seen the first time. This time I could see. And everything I saw in this life review, starting with the day I was born until the day I had died, was not at all what I had seen before; this time these were things that were important to God, not important to man. And they were not all those accomplishments that I talked about before. These were things like love and acts of kindness -- things I couldn't even remember I had done. Befriending someone that everyone was mean to, or a neglected animal -- I helped an animal, giving money to a homeless person when I really didn't have money to give. Helping someone cross the street -- an elderly person. Every single action, word, thought, feeling was all about love. We lived all of those series of events just like... it was happening for the very first time. I lived it again. And I felt so much unconditional love from God as we were reliving these series of events together...

Watch The Companion Video
thepurposeoflife-nde.com/videos/

Learn About Near-Death Experiencer Erica McKenzie
thepurposeoflife-nde.com/contents/

THE PURPOSE OF LIFE

- 12 -

Everything Is Made Of LOVE! *
Near-Death-Like Experiencer Mary Deioma

I want to share my story with you to let you know that this is something that is possible.

And for those thousands or millions of people that have already experienced something like this, I can be another validation for you.

I was lucky enough to experience something very special. I had a moment of enlightenment; a moment of actual, direct contact with God.

It happened at a time in my life when I was experiencing a personal tragedy. I was driving down the road and I felt so much pain in my heart that my heart was breaking. I was angry! I felt like I had done everything right. I felt like I followed all the guidance that I received from God. I felt like I had made the right choices. But still the situation was heartbreaking.

THE PURPOSE OF LIFE

So I'm driving along and I'm really angry with God and finally I decided to ask myself, "What would Mother Teresa do in this situation?"

And it came to me immediately, "Mother Teresa would love anyway."

And then I asked, "What would Jesus do in this situation?"

And it came to me immediately, "Jesus would forgive his enemies. People that hurt me, I forgive them."

And then I asked, "What would Muhammad do?"

And it came to me immediately, "Muhammad would submit."

And I understood it in a way that I never understood it before. I understood that meant to turn my life over to God. To humbly ask God to help me; to take this pain from me. And I did. I imagined my heart going out to God.

In that moment, a beam of pure white came out of the sky and came down and touched me on my shoulder. I was so filled with love, it's impossible to describe how much love there was in that moment. All the love of the world filled my whole entire body. Every cell in my body was completely infused with this love. It was the love of a parent for their precious child.

In the same moment, I recognized that I always knew this. That this truth was always there for me. I was remembering and not just learning something new. I was remembering "I AM part of this love! I AM God and God is me!"

It doesn't really convey the truth to say the words. It doesn't come close.

As this beam touched me, suddenly I was viewing this scene of the road, as I was driving, from three different places. I was seeing it from my body. I was seeing it from the passenger's seat (from the passenger's seat, I could see it from my intellect). I was observing, clearly, the edges of the beam and thinking, "that's not light!" The view is at the top and it came to a point on my shoulder and it came through the window and it touched me. It had contact... It wasn't until later that I could really process that information. But I was taking it all in.

And from behind, the back passenger's seat, I was all in love; just emotion; an incredible amount of emotion.

And then my soul went out of my heart. My soul went up the beam and as it went up the beam I felt so connected to all souls. As I reached the top of the beam, I rippled out in concentric circles and I became one with every soul on the planet.

THE PURPOSE OF LIFE

Then my focus shifted and I became one with all the trees on the planet. Physically, I could feel that I was in a tree. And I was looking at another tree in the forest, which was me, looking back at me. It was so incredible. And then, I was all the grass and I was looking at a blade of grass next to me that was me looking back at me. It was amazing.

Then my focus shifted and I was a rock on a mountain. I was the Earth. And that really surprised me because I never imagined that inanimate objects are filled with God Consciousness.

Then my focus shifted again and it was all of the entire universe -- the complete, entire universe. So humongous!

At the same time, I don't know how, but I could see the smallest, tiniest particle. What the universe is made out of. It was this massive, uniform field of particles. At the tiniest level, the tiniest particle, smaller than anything we can record, it was pure white, sort of a radiant light. This particle was pure energy. But more than that, this particle that everything in the entire universe is made out of, is LOVE! A tangible love that is the stuff of God. It just blew me away! It was awesome.

I went beyond the universe into pure consciousness. I've heard it called The Void, but that doesn't come close to describing what it was. It's not anything you can describe, which is so frustrating, because I so want to let you know what it's like. It is pure potential; pure consciousness prior to actualization. It doesn't look like anything. It's outside of time and space. It isn't close to anything you can describe in the physical universe. But it was so amazing. So full of love. So incredible.

Whatever pain! Woo! That was gone! [Laughing] There was no pain left over.

I realized that at the same time all of this was happening, I was driving along the road. The whole thing didn't take more than a second and a half.

There was a sign, a building next to the exit that I was just getting off of, that was illuminated in the bookstore. I got it that God wanted me to go to that bookstore. So I did. I made that split-second decision -- Oh, this really happened! -- and I turned the wheel and I went on the exit to get to the bookstore. And I went to the bookstore.

And then I was back into myself -- totally, completely realizing myself as normal [laughing]. Now here I am in the bookstore and I'm like, "OK, now what?!"

THE PURPOSE OF LIFE

Watch The Companion Video
thepurposeoflife-nde.com/videos/

Learn About Near-Death-Like Experiencer Mary Deioma
thepurposeoflife-nde.com/contents/

NDEs On The Importance Of Plants, Animals & The Earth
the-formula.org/ndes-on-the-importance-of-caring-for-plants-animals-the-earth/

- 13 -

The Light Has A Fantastic Sense Of Humor *
Near-Death Experiencer Andy Petro

I was pulled out of my body and all of a sudden, I looked down, and I could see my body stuck in the mud... No longer am I cold and freezing and stuck in the mud, but I'm warm and I'm filled with a love and a peace that I cannot explain. So in less than a microsecond, from freezing, cold, horrible pain, I was filled with love and peace and happiness and smiles. And as I looked opposite from my body, looked up into the tunnel, there I saw a light. The light was so bright that it was brighter than ten thousand suns. I immediately said, "this should be burning my retinas." But it wasn't. It was a gentle, but powerful light. It was pulling me; it was pulling me like a gentle magnet. Closer and closer. And the closer I got, the more I was filled with the ecstasy, with the love, with the unconditional love of me, as Andy.

As I got closer to the light, all of a sudden, I popped into a giant sphere. It was about the size of a basketball colosseum. I was suspended in the middle of this sphere. All around me, in all parts of the sphere -- up, down, sideways, left, right, all over -- were miniature motion pictures of my lives and what was going on. And I could see, I could touch, I could feel, I could sense every emotion that was taking place in all of those lifetimes. When I would concentrate on one, I would immediately be there; I would be reliving what I had lived and I would remember the reliving. Then I would think about another area. Then I would pop into another movie. And I would do this for some period of time, but you have to understand that when you are in the eternal now, time doesn't make any sense. So, it isn't time like yesterday, today, tomorrow; it's happening all the time. I was there for an extended period using Earth terms and then all of a sudden, I popped out of the sphere and now I'm in front of The Light.

And The Light is so warm and so glowing and so forgiving. The Light has no judgement. There was no condemnation. There was no blaming. No shame. There was nothing but love and acceptance. And The Light was viewing me. The Light knew everything I had ever thought, done, or will do.

It knew everything. And The Light welcomed me. The Light said, "Andy, don't be afraid." And I was impressed... The Light knew me and called me by my name! Called me Andy. I thought that was pretty good. Then The Light said, "Andy I love you." And then The Light said, "Andy we love you."

Now when The Light said "Andy, we love you," I looked in back of The Light -- and The Light was a huge, giant form that I have never seen on Earth and I cannot describe, but I recognized It and I can see it right now in my mind's eye. And as The Light said to me "Andy, we love you," in back of The Light were billions and billions and billions of other lights. And all of them knew me. And all of them said in a giant chorus, "Welcome Home Andy!" And I said out loud, "I'm Home. At last I'm Home!"

And The Light welcomed me; The Light absorbed me into The Light. So I was part of The Light. Once I was in The Light, I knew everything The Light knew. I knew all about the universe. I knew everything about flowers, about plants, about asteroids, about suns, about novas -- everything. I didn't have a question for The Light. Why? Because I knew all the answers. I had nothing to ask. And we laughed and we played. And by the way, The Light has a fantastic sense of humor! We reviewed some of the really silly things that I did in my lifetime and we would be laughing at how serious I took them. Because life down here is an illusion. It's a game. Don't take it so seriously. The Light has a wonderful sense of humor.

And we're laughing and we're talking and we're just having a great time and then The Light says to me, "Andy, you have to go back."

Now, I'm not going back! I said to The Light, "I don't think so. I'm Home. I'm staying."

And then The Light said to me for the second time, "Andy, you're going back."

And I said, "No, you don't understand. I don't want to go back into that body. I don't want to go back on Earth. I'm Home here in The Light."

And then The Light said for the third time, "Andy, you're going back." And as soon as I heard the "k" from the "back" I was pushed back into my body, filled with pain and anxiety... I was now on the beach and my friends were pushing the water out of my lungs and I was coughing the water out and I was completely conscious. And I was crying. All of my classmates thought I was crying from the pain of drowning. But I was crying because I was no longer in The Light. I was back in my body. I was back on Earth. I wanted to be in The Light..."

Watch The Companion Video
thepurposeoflife-nde.com/videos/

Learn About Near-Death Experiencer Andy Petro
thepurposeoflife-nde.com/contents/

Heavenly Humor In Near-Death Experiences
the-formula.org/heavenly-humor/

- 14 -

The Funniest Thought In The World

Near-Death-Like Experiencer John K

I became aware the God I was experiencing was not just a life force, or some impersonal consciousness, but God had a personality, an integrity like the father I had never known. God had a sense of humor! He and I both laughed at the thought of me questioning His existence. It seemed to me the absolutely funniest thought in the world, and we laughed at the thought of it. I realized that I was the shadow, and He was the reality. The very idea that I would question His existence was a source of laughter for God and me. I was sobbing, overcome by the sheer amount of love that swept through me and over me, and laughing at the same time.

THE PURPOSE OF LIFE

Learn About Near-Death Experiencer John K
thepurposeoflife-nde.com/contents/

Heavenly Humor In Near-Death Experiences
the-formula.org/heavenly-humor/

The Cable Guys *

Near-Death Experiencer Amy Call

I remember after my experience I had the simplest situation where two cable guys showed up at my house... What I discovered was the Divine having a sense of humor. Things are funny. The two cable guys show up at the house and they were wearing their uniforms for work and they were there to hook up the cable for the TV. My husband had made an appointment and he had to go to work right after my NDE... He was very busy taking care of the family, and so I was at home in this state with kids just trying to figure out how to function. And the cable guys show up and when I opened the door, I saw them how the Divine sees them, and I couldn't stop laughing. I was trying not to be rude, but to me they looked like -- if you imagine little kids going into the closet and trying clothes on and trying to look really serious and showing up at the door and be like, "We're the cable guys." I can't describe it. I was like, "Oh, OK." I brought them in and they were just really serious about their job like, "We're here to hook up the TV." To me it was just so funny because I was so disconnected from things like television, and watching football, or sitcoms... I just didn't realize that this appointment was coming and while they were hooking it up, they were asking me really simple questions like, "OK, so what channel do you want? Do you want ESPN? Do you want the cartoon channel?" Everything they were asking me was busting me up.

I got to where I felt like I was being rude because they have an important job. There's nothing that isn't important. Everything that people do is a part of their own vital experience and it's all beautiful really. It's just that it felt totally different to me. I had to actually -- I told them I'm really sorry; I think I'm sick or something. And one of the guys said, "Did you take some NyQuil?" And I was wiping the tears and blowing my nose and I finally said, "You know what, you guys can hook up anything you want because I need to leave the room." And so, I had to leave because I knew at some point it was going to look like I was being rude...

I saw people from then on the way we see toddlers when they're playing. I see that despite how we age here -- we get older and we take ourselves seriously and we think, you know, I have this important thing I'm doing -- but the Divine is like: "Lighten up. It's OK, you can lighten up." I tend to be so serious from what I came from. I worry so much. I thought things were so serious and I wanted to please God and I prayed so much and now through the Divine I was saying that it's totally OK to just have fun and laugh. I was laughing so much, I was wheezing...

AS REVEALED BY NEAR-DEATH EXPERIENCES

Watch The Companion Video
thepurposeoflife-nde.com/videos/

Learn About Near-Death Experiencer Amy Call
thepurposeoflife-nde.com/contents/

Heavenly Humor In Near-Death Experiences
the-formula.org/heavenly-humor/

THE PURPOSE OF LIFE

- 16 -

I Don't Want To Go Back! *
Near-Death Experiencer Howard Storm

First Excerpt:

I never saw God, and I was not in heaven. It was way out in the suburbs, and these are the things that they showed me. We talked for a long time, about many things, and then I looked at myself. When I saw me, I was glowing. I was radiant. I was becoming beautiful -- not nearly as beautiful as them -- but I had a certain sparkle that I never had before.

Not being ready to face the Earth again, I told them that I wished to be with them forever. I said, "I'm ready, I'm ready to be like you and be here forever. This is great. I love it. I love you. You're wonderful."

I knew that they loved me and knew everything about me. I knew that everything was going to be okay from now on. I asked if I could get rid of my body, which was definitely a hindrance, and become a being like them with the powers they had shown me. They said, "No, you have to go back."

They explained to me that I was very underdeveloped and that it would be of great benefit to return to my physical existence to learn. In my human life I would have an opportunity to grow so that the next time I was with them I would be more compatible. I would need to develop important characteristics to become like them and to be involved with the work that they do. Responding that I couldn't go back, I tried to argue with them, and I observed that if I bear that thought -- the thought that I might wind up in the pit again -- I pled with them to stay.

My friends then said, "Do you think that we expect you to be perfect, after all the love we feel for you, even after you were on Earth blaspheming God, and treating everyone around you like dirt? And this, despite the fact that we were sending people to try and help you, to teach you the truth? Do you really think we would be apart from you now?"

I asked them, "But what about my own sense of failure? You've shown me how I can be better, and I'm sure I can't live up to that. I'm not that good." Some of my self-centeredness welled up and I said, "No way. I'm not going back."

They said, "There are people who care about you; your wife, your children, your mother and father. You should go back for them. Your children need your help."

I said, "You can help them. If you make me go back there are things that just won't work. If I go back there and make mistakes I won't be able to stand it because you've shown me I could be more loving and more compassionate and I'll forget. I'll be mean to someone or I'll do something awful to someone. I just know it's going to happen because I'm a human being. I'm going to blow it and I won't be able to stand it. I'll feel so bad I'll want to kill myself and I can't do that because life is precious. I might just go catatonic. So you can't send me back."

They assured me that mistakes are an acceptable part of being human. "Go," they said, "and make all the mistakes you want. Mistakes are how you learn." As long as I tried to do what I knew was right, they said, I would be on the right path. If I made a mistake, I should fully recognize it as a mistake, then put it behind me and simply try not to make the same mistake again. The important thing is to try one's best, keep one's standards of goodness and truth, and not to compromise these to win people's approval.

"But," I said, "mistakes make me feel bad."

They said, "We love you the way you are, mistakes and all. And you can feel our forgiveness. You can feel our love any time you want to."

I said, "I don't understand. How do I do that?"

"Just turn inward," they said. "Just ask for our love and we'll give it to you if you ask from the heart."

They advised me to recognize when I made a mistake and ask for forgiveness. Before I even got the words out of my mouth, I would be forgiven but, I would have to accept the forgiveness. My belief in the principal of forgiveness must be real, and I would have to know that forgiveness was given. Confessing, either in public or in private, that I had made a mistake, I should then ask for forgiveness. After that, it would be an insult to them if I didn't accept the forgiveness. I shouldn't continue to go around with a sense of guilt, and I should not repeat errors. I should learn from my mistakes.

"But," I said, "how will I know what is the right choice? How will I know what you want me to do?"

They replied, "We want you to do what you want to do. That means making choices, and there isn't necessarily any right choice. There are a spectrum of possibilities, and you should make the best choice you can from those possibilities. If you do that, we will be there helping you."

I didn't give in easily. I argued that back there everything was full of problems and that everything I could possibly want was here. I questioned my ability to accomplish anything they would consider important in my world. They said the world is a beautiful expression of the Supreme Being. One can find beauty or ugliness depending on what one directs one's mind toward. They explained that the subtle and complex development of our world was beyond my comprehension, but that I would be a suitable instrument for the Creator. Every part of the creation, they explained, is infinitely interesting because it is a manifestation of the Creator. A very important opportunity for me would be to explore this world with wonder and enjoyment. They never gave me a direct mission or purpose. Could I build a shrine or cathedral for God? They said those monuments were for humanity. They wanted me to live my life to love people, not things. I told them I wasn't good enough to represent what I had just experienced with them on a worldly level. They assured me I would be given appropriate help whenever I might need it. All I had to do is ask.

The luminous beings, my teachers, were very convincing. I was also acutely aware that not far away was the Great Being, whom I knew to be the Creator. They never said, "He wants it this way," but that was implied behind everything they said. I didn't want to argue too much because the Great Entity was so wonderful and so awesome. The love that emanated was overwhelming.

Presenting my biggest argument against coming back into the world, I told them that it would break my heart, and I would die, if I had to leave them and their love. Going back would be so cruel, I said, that I couldn't stand it. I mentioned that the world was filled with hate and competition, and I didn't want to return to that maelstrom. I couldn't bear to leave them. My friends observed that they had never been apart from me. I explained that I hadn't been aware of their presence, and if I went back I, again, wouldn't know they were there. Explaining how to communicate with them, they told me to get myself quiet, inside, and to ask for their love; then that love would come, and I would know they were there. They said, "You won't be away from us. We are with you. We have always been with you. We always will be right with you all the time."

I said, "But how do I know that? You tell me that, but when I go back there it's just going to be a nice theory."

They said, "Any time you need us we'll be there for you."

I said, "You mean you will just appear?"

They said, "No, no. We're not going to intervene in your life in any big way unless you need us. We are just going to be there and you will feel our presence, you will feel our love."

After that explanation I ran out of arguments, and I said I thought I could go back. And, just like that, I was back..

AS REVEALED BY NEAR-DEATH EXPERIENCES

Second Excerpt:

My final argument -- this was the biggie; this was the ace I've been keeping up my sleeve -- I said, "You can't send me back."

They said, "Why?"

"I've never known anybody that loved me like you did. I've never known anybody that knew me like you do because you know me better than I know me... If you send me back, it will kill me. I will die of a broken heart."

"You're not paying attention. Has there been a moment in your life when we have ever been a part from you, when you have ever been alone or separate from us?"

"No, but I never saw you, I never talked to you, I never felt you. Is it going to be like that when I go back?"

And they said it's going to be exactly like that.

"Well, it's kind of like being alone when you can't see, hear, taste, touch the person that's with you. They're not there. It feels lonely... That would kill me, in loneliness, to be a part from you."

They said, "There is a way to get in touch with us."

THE PURPOSE OF LIFE

"How do you do that?"

"Be still, get quiet, talk to us, tell us everything you want to say. Then be really quiet and still and invite our love into your heart and you'll know that we are right there and you'll know our love right there."

This works. It really works...

Watch The Companion Video
thepurposeoflife-nde.com/videos/

Learn About Near-Death Experiencer Howard Storm
thepurposeoflife-nde.com/contents/

You Can Do Better *
Near-Death Experiencer Mary Jo Rapini

God held me... I don't remember if my whole body was in His arms or what... no recognition of that. I knew it was God because He was an omnipotent being. Not like a person... much less limited in form. I did not see God but felt Him through my skin. He spoke through all of my senses. He called me by name and told me I could not stay. I protested. I told Him all of my services on Earth -- working 24/7, not much money for my work, a good wife, a good mother. I did not want to leave this place. Then God asked me... He said, "Let me ask you one question. Have you ever loved another person the way you have been loved here?"

The love I had received in there was so overpowering... I had never felt anything like it, so I answered God honestly. I said, "No... it is impossible... I am just a human, you are God."

He gave me the illusion of a sweet protective chuckle. He then said, "Mary, you can do better."

THE PURPOSE OF LIFE

Watch The Companion Video
thepurposeoflife-nde.com/videos/

Learn About Near-Death Experiencer Mary Jo Rapini
thepurposeoflife-nde.com/contents/

- 18 -

Part Of You Is Choosing & Participating
Near-Death Experiencer Naomi

From Dr. Laurin Bellg's book, Near Death in the ICU: Stories from Patients Near Death and Why We Should Listen to Them

It seemed no sooner than I'd arrived there that my mother told me I couldn't stay, that I had to go back. That really upset me... My husband, he's a good man, but he's not always an easy man to live with. He's pretty hard to please, so I really didn't want to come back, quite honestly. I don't want him to know that, but it would have been so much easier to stay there where I was, with my mother. So I was not happy at all when she told me I had to go back. I was pretty sad really. I even tried pleading with her to let me stay. I told her, "It's my life, I should get to choose. I should have a say-so."

Then she told me, "It's not that you don't get to choose. Part of you, in fact, is choosing and participating in this decision. It would be easy for you to choose to stay here, but you understand on a level you can't quite comprehend just now that there is more from your family relationships you need to experience and learn. And more they need to learn from you. When choosing is not an act of escape but an act of completion, then you will stay."

I knew what she said was true, but in that moment, it didn't make it any easier...

Near Death In The ICU
thepurposeoflife-nde.com/books/

- 19 -

Why Am I So Depressed?
Near-Death-Like Experiencer Krystal Winzer

I asked the voice, "Are you God?"

"Yes."

The voice sounded masculine, but it was as if a waterfall or mountain could talk, if that makes sense. It sounded like no human voice I have ever heard before.

I had to ask this: "Does Jesus exist?"

The answer I got was "Jesus is God."

I realized that must be who I was talking to, the spirit of Jesus. I asked again to confirm.

"Jesus is God?!" I asked.

"Yes."

THE PURPOSE OF LIFE

This is going to sound silly, but I let it slip that I hated Christianity. And this voice of God laughed! God has a great sense of humor! Then I realized I didn't hate Christianity and definitely did not hate Jesus, I just did not like some of his followers.

I asked this question, "Why am I so depressed all of the time?"

"You forgot that I love you."

As I spoke with God, His love for me, this intense love that I can't explain, was making me feel powerful. I think for a little, while God let me see through His eyes, I suddenly felt love for everyone.

Learn About Near-Death-Like Experiencer Krystal Winzer
thepurposeoflife-nde.com/contents/

Other People Who Encountered Jesus
encounters-with-jesus.org/encounters/

Bring The Light Into This World *

Near-Death Experiencer Anne Horn

He looked down at me and he said, "you're not supposed to be here. It's not time for you to be here."

I remember looking up at him and saying, "but I want to be here"... With all my heart, I wanted to be there. I wanted to go Home. I was happy.

He took a pause and... you could see him thinking about something and deciding whether to say something. And with that... there was a picture placed in my head of a memory of my original agreement of why I had come to Earth to begin with. It was like I remembered, and I went, "Oh, right. Right..."

One of the things that bothers me so tremendously about the metaphysical movement, in lieu of my experience and in lieu of what I was shown... if there is any message I can give, it's not about meditating and leaving your body and taking your Light

THE PURPOSE OF LIFE

Being out of this Earth. Indeed, not. It is about bringing The Light into this Earth. Stay here. Be an anchor. Let The Light come in through you into this world. Don't abandon this world. We need you. We need you here. We need you to be present. And we need you to be open, with an open heart... Everybody must be open. To bring this new age in, it is about opening your heart and letting it sing through you. It is coming! And it is a matter of all of us. Just open your heart and let It come in. Don't leave. Don't meditate and think this place is a bad place and we're going to get out of here. This is a wonderful place. And it's going to get even more wonderful. You are here to anchor The Light so It can come into this dimension and be here.

Watch The Companion Video
thepurposeoflife-nde.com/videos/

Learn About Near-Death Experiencer Anne Horn
thepurposeoflife-nde.com/contents/

Hold The Energy Of The Light *

Near-Death Experiencer Ellyn Dye

We all know that we came back with a mission. Most of us don't know what it was at the time, but we know we had one. You spend a lot of time trying to figure out what that was. At different times since then, I've come up with ideas as to what my mission was, but now I think my mission and everybody's mission is to be here, in three dimensions, in this time, in this space, and to hold the energy of The Light of God. Just hold it. We don't have to do anything. Just hold that energy. If we hold it, we help other people around us find that energy and feel that energy. Humanity is changing. Humanity is evolving and this is the time. All you have to remember is there is nothing out there to fear. You are a divine, powerful being. We all are. We are all part of God. We are all part of love. That's who we are. We are the heart of God. We are here to bring that to planet Earth. To create Heaven on Earth. We can do it. In love. That's why we are here.

THE PURPOSE OF LIFE

Watch The Companion Video
thepurposeoflife-nde.com/videos/

Learn About Near-Death Experiencer Ellyn Dye
thepurposeoflife-nde.com/contents/

God Becoming Us
Near-Death Experiencer Mellen-Thomas Benedict

Creation is God exploring God's Self through every way imaginable, in an ongoing, infinite exploration through every one of us. Through every piece of hair on your head, through every leaf on every tree, through every atom, God is exploring God's Self, the great "I AM."

...

The other side is not all it is cracked up to be. There's a lot you can't do on the other side. There's a perfect combination though. A body without spirit is a wasteland and a spirit without a body is a wasteland. And we are the perfect matrix of body and spirit. With body and spirit, you can have it all.

...

The body is the most magnificent light being there is. The body is a universe of incredible light. Spirit is not pushing us to dissolve this body. That is not what is happening. Stop trying to become God; God is becoming you. Here.

...

God gave everything to us, everything is here -- this is where it's at. What we are into now is God's exploration of God through us. People are so busy trying to become God that they ought to realize that we are already God and God is becoming us. That's what it is really about. When I realized this, I was finished with The Void, and wanted to return to this creation...

Learn About Near-Death Experiencer Mellen-Thomas Benedict
thepurposeoflife-nde.com/videos/

- 23 -

We Come Here To Learn About Ourselves *
Near-Death Experiencer Ryan Rampton

I want to talk to you today about why we came to this Earth. These are things I learned in Heaven. So number one, why did we come here? What is our purpose? Did we come here to be tested and tried and try to prove how righteous we are to God; keep a list of commandments or things like this? Is that why we came here? No. That is not why we came here.

We came here for one thing. And that was to learn about ourselves. That's it. We came to find out who you are and how you respond to different things.

So for example one of the main things we came here for was to learn joy. We didn't know what joy was before. When we were up in heaven, we knew one thing. We knew love. That's what God was. And we learned different concepts and we learned how to do different things, but we didn't know joy and we wanted to know joy. God told us: the only way to know joy is to know sorrow. So we had to come down to this physical realm that He made, so we could learn about sorrow, so we could have joy.

So we're not down here to prove anything to God. We're not down here to earn His love. We're not down here to do certain things to make ourselves righteous in His eyes. All those things are great, all those things are awesome, but that's not why we came down here.

We came down here to experience opposition. We came down here to feel the opposite.

For example, we would never know what a great health felt like if you'd never been sick. You would never know what a wonderful day in Hawaii would be if you didn't live in a winter environment. You'd go to Hawaii in the middle of the winter and you're going, "Yeah, this is awesome!" And the guy on the beach that's local is like, "What's the big deal, man? It's this way every day."

So it's the opposition that defines us. It's the space between things that creates form. All of these things need each other. We need opposition to even know who we are.

For example, when the Lord showed me my spirit, before I came to this Earth, I saw this amazing, glorious, just breathtakingly beautiful, amazing warrior. The armament, and the clothing, and the raiment that I had on was so amazing and I was just breathtaking to behold. So I come down here and I end up being in this little, sick, weak body that spends the first seven years of its life in an oxygen tent, clinging on to life. I was skinny and even when I got married. My wife actually weighed more than I did... So I learned what it was like to be weak. I learned what it was like to have shame. I learned what it was like to have all these things. This opposition made me into who I am today.

Even the mistakes I've made. Even all the bad things I've done in my life. All the sins. All the terrible things. They helped form me into who I am today.

Watch The Companion Video
thepurposeoflife-nde.com/videos/

Learn About Near-Death Experiencer Ryan Rampton
thepurposeoflife-nde.com/contents/

THE PURPOSE OF LIFE

- 24 -

True Learning Happens In The Body *
Near-Death Experiencer Amy Call

True learning happens in the body. This is a big deal to me personally because so much of my life was about wanting to escape the body and wanting that for other people. I also grew up hearing that when you die you get to take off that glove; you get to be free and so I thought that here [in this world] is the more negative, that there [on the other side of life] is the more positive. The understanding in this place -- as hard as it is to see and understand -- is that true learning happens within the body because when we are in experience, in this form, there is something that evolves within us at the level of the soul that makes the body an important part of the whole. It isn't that one is good and one is bad. The two work together in an important way. That was very healing for me personally, to come to a better understanding.

THE PURPOSE OF LIFE

Watch The Companion Video
thepurposeoflife-nde.com/videos/

Learn About Near-Death Experiencer Amy Call
thepurposeoflife-nde.com/contents/

- 25 -

A Place To Test Ourselves Under Pressure

Near-Death Experiencer Jean R

I was told that people choose to be born into whichever religion or group that will help them achieve the lessons they are sent here to learn. I was told that the Earth is like a big school, a place where you can apply spiritual lessons learned and test yourself, under pressure, to see if you can actually "live" what you already know you should do. Basically, the Earth is a place to walk the walk and literally live the way it should be done. It was made clear to me that some people come to the Earth to work on only one aspect of themselves, while others come to work on several aspects. Then there are others who come to not only work on their own nature, but also to help the world as a whole.

The other side does not have the physical pressures that having a body has. Here on Earth, you must feed and clothe that body and provide shelter for it from the elements. You are under continual pressure of some sort, to make decisions that have a spiritual base. You are taught on the other side what you are supposed to do, but can you LIVE it under these pressures on Earth. From what I saw and heard there, it is all about relationships and taking care of each other. Perfection is not expected of people, but learning is expected and considered good progress.

All of our experiences in a lifetime tend to follow some sort of pattern and often will recreate the same lessons, only in a different way, and under various circumstances. This is how you know what you are here to learn and test. If you examine the patterns, certain themes will become clear.

I was shown a library filled with gold covered books. These are the lives of people on Earth where their life plan is laid out and what they hope to achieve through certain key experiences. From what I was shown, people have free choice as to how to get to these preset key experiences. They can take a meandering path of experiences or a more direct route, but there are certain events that are preset and will happen, no matter what. Each of those key events are benchmarks and one's reactions to them will show how much they have learned and what more needs to be done or learned.

Learn About Near-Death Experiencer Jean R
thepurposeoflife-nde.com/contents/

– 26 –

The Ultimate Theme Park

Near-Death Experiencer Duane S

As I was shown around, it was explained to me how most of our celestial, eternal knowledge is blanked-out during our chosen life spans on Earth. We must temporarily forget most of what our Higher Self already knows so we can immerse ourselves in the roles we have chosen to play. Furthermore, they said that it might take a while for all my knowledge and memories to return. To ease the transition back into this realm, I was told to think of my time on Earth as an extended visit to the ultimate theme park. Consider it a place with thrilling rides and various adventures that I could choose to experience or not. I was also reminded that the reason we leave the celestial realm at all was for the excitement, variety, adventure, and entertainment that different incarnations offer. However, to take all our celestial knowledge with us on our various adventures would have ruined the very experience that we had chosen to live. Someone there said that I should think of our trips to other realms as choosing a new novel to read. I can choose a new book, depending on what I am in the mood for. Furthermore, if I knew every turn and twist of the story, line by line, prior to reading it, it would spoil the fun.

As one entity jokingly remarked, "If the eternal, divine part of us grows tired of singing and playing harps, there are thousands of other universes created for our spiritual growth, amusement, and entertainment..."

As my orientation went on, they explained how on that celestial side of the veil, anything we desire is instantaneously provided. We just need to feel the desire. However, within lies the reason for all the realms outside of Heaven. Having everything we want all the time develops within us a desire for variety and change for a challenge. It would be like a game in which everyone was a winner. Soon, the game would become boring, and we would look for another, more challenging one...

Learn About Near-Death Experiencer Duane S
thepurposeoflife-nde.com/contents/

- 27 -

Life Is Really Exciting *
Near-Death Experiencer Natalie Sudman

We can be over there anytime and infinitely; forever and forever, for a long time, and it's so easy and it's so beautiful, but this life here is really exciting from the other side. And it's pretty quick. So dig in and enjoy it... A lot of spiritual messages seem to be "deny the body, these emotions are bad emotions, these things are not holy" and I don't think that's true. From my experience, everything is holy. Here is there. We didn't come here just to experience all the happy things. We also came here to experience the difficult emotions because we learn from those and they enrich us in ways that we really can't get when we are out of body, when we are in our Whole Selves. If we could get those out there, we wouldn't be here. From that perspective, it's very exciting to participate in any kind of emotions, and any kind of situation. It's an adventure. It's amazing. It's beautiful.... It's a kick. It can be really fun.

THE PURPOSE OF LIFE

Watch The Companion Video
thepurposeoflife-nde.com/videos/

Learn About Near-Death Experiencer Natalie Sudman
thepurposeoflife-nde.com/contents/

- 28 -

The Truth Is Hidden While We Are Alive

Near-Death Experiencer Amphianda Baskett

It is rarely fully satisfying to get the answers to specific questions about the purpose of life, or why we suffer. I believe a huge reason why answers are not satisfying is because this deepest truth is hidden from us while we are alive. I think we can sort of KNOW the ultimate purpose, and yet still NOT KNOW. It's almost impossible to describe. In my near-death experience, it could not have been more obvious or more simple: Our purpose is to overcome fear, each one of us. We are supposed to utilize faith. We are supposed to let go, let God, trust God. The whole point is LOVE; to remember to choose LOVE instead of fear. It's hard to see these truths while we are wrestling around in the "muck" of life. To be simply given the answer when the question is asked almost never works as a magic bullet to cure life's ills. It seems there is some kind of struggle we are supposed to endure, and answering the question will not take that struggle away. The struggle we endure, we endure TOGETHER, and some say it is for the expansion of the universe. Even I, years after my experience, seek the answer while knowing on some level what the answer is. I think this is as it is supposed to be. We are supposed to seek, and seek again, each time coming to a deeper understanding.

Learn About Near-Death Experiencer Amphianda Baskett
thepurposeoflife-nde.com/contents/

It's All Good *

Near-Death Experiencer Amy Call

First Excerpt:

In my NDE I came to understand that most of us have lived much, much longer than we could even fathom. That our lives which feel so very long are infinitesimal when placed in the whole picture... which for that matter, cannot even be framed. I was shown how every single individual through their own free will chooses paths that MATHEMATICALLY take them to the circumstances of their next existence or life; that NOTHING at all sits in accident or chaos; that every single aspect of our lives are ruled by NATURAL laws that we placed ourselves in; that in a sense, we create our own worlds. I was shown how one can never assume either, that if someone lives a life of suffering that this is because of "evil" deeds. Many may CHOOSE a life of suffering because of what it awakens in them... or to help another, etc. We can NEVER EVER assume that we can be accurate in guessing why each being lives the life they live. I cannot describe the relief, the refreshing, peaceful balm this knowledge was for me. To finally gather this truth that I'd yearned for all of my life -- that all is good; that there is sense and beauty all around; that no one is just "free-falling" as it had seemed before; that God doesn't just get to toy with us as He pleases with random ideas of tests, including rewards and punishments that just depend upon His current mood or mindset. While in this experience, out in the vast expanse of stars and planets, moons, and knowledge, I knew complete trust for what felt like the first time. This was bliss for me. I had lived in fear and distrust and panic for 30 years.

...

My Guide stood by at a certain time... and he lovingly stayed as my support while I had a kind of life review. I never felt chastised at all, even though I know I've been very cruel at times and have hurt many people. I've lost my temper in horrible ways and I have had great trouble with forgiveness, and yet, I felt only love and understanding through the entire life review. What it felt like was that I was being given the opportunity and the gift of being able to stand back and more fully understand and love myself. I was able to feel exactly what others around me had felt during my life. I understood how everything I did and said and even thought had touched others around me in one way or another. I was able to even enter the minds and emotional centers of many who had been around me, and understand where they were coming from in their own thinking; how their own personal views and life experiences had brought them to the places where they stood. I felt their struggling and their fears; their desperate need for love and approval -- and more than anything, I could feel how child-like everyone was. With every person I viewed, including myself, I was able to see and feel with a Higher Mind and Eye. And the feeling I had toward everyone was nothing less than what a loving mother would feel for her children at toddler age.

It was actually comical at times. I could feel how the "Elders" as I will call them (those who are Helpers on the other side, who have mastered themselves in many or all ways, and help work with us) see us and find so much humor in the way we do things. It might seem brutally annoying to consider when we are in the midst of a great argument or drama that is playing out in our lives that the Elders view these things very much like when a mother sees her two-year-old scream and cry and bop another child on the head with a stuffed animal. The mother doesn't want her child to "fall apart" and become hysterical and cry. She feels for her child, but at the same time, she sees a little bit of comedy in how seriously the child takes what is usually a trivial drama. She continues to love her child and thinks the world of it, hoping it will go on enjoying the day, living and learning.

This was a big light bulb moment for me, because I had entertained the dark idea, during my life, that every little less than perfect action of mine, was being watched "by God," and judged with anger or great sadness. I felt constant guilt for my mistakes and belabored over the dread of "being watched" with severe or at least very stern eyes. I wanted to please, and I believed that I was so often falling short. This had been a maddening way to live. So getting the chance to view others from a much Higher Frequency was wonderful, to say the least. And knowing how much love I felt as I watched or sensed others in their personal situations, made me want to live more in joy rather than guilt and worry. No one was mad at me.

I was able to explore the mind or energetic pattern of one of my life's sworn enemies -- someone I couldn't imagine forgiving for what I'd witnessed. And yet, coming back from my NDE, I could feel nothing more than such a flood of Love for this woman that I dived in at the chance to write her a letter and tell her how much I loved her, and to ask for forgiveness for the energetic weight I might have held over her from my own dark thoughts and anger. She could have been my own firstborn. That is how much I adored her at that time. Because I was able to feel the Divine Love for her that God feels toward her, I, too, couldn't help but love her in a similar way. It was such a surprisingly marvelous feeling to relinquish the burden of my own anger and judgments -- much of which I hadn't even carried consciously most of my years.

Surveying all of this, I want to note, that I felt a Higher part of me that had compassion for the me that was so ignorant and juvenile. It seemed to understand what I was working with, in every detail, and it only wanted for my joy. I felt that toward my own self, if that makes any sense. I desired to have my lower self Awaken, and to be filled with Love and Joy. I wanted for my lower, child-like self to be kinder, to be more Conscious, and to find Peace.

I am forever grateful for my life review and what I took from it.

...

I came back with this Knowing that despite what SEEMED "good" or "bad" before... it now became united to be only "Good." Because I trusted and knew that everything was in its right place... even when people made decisions that I didn't agree with, I still felt that in the overall picture, it was ALL "Good." I had this knowing as well, that there was the essence or spark of the Highest (as I'll refer to "God") in EVERYTHING. In every mineral, vegetable, animal, human, and beyond... I just knew that the Highest waited within everything to expand and create and grow and experience. I lost all desire to analyze everything in life, as I'd done before through religious examples, by trying to judge every little thing as being either "good" or "bad." I wasn't concerned. We are all just consciousness experiencing life, and learning how to love, create, and develop to the Highest we can be. I knew to choose what felt right for me and to trust more. That when something felt unjust or imbalanced, to do what I could to work toward harmony, but to not worry about that which I had no control over. I know that eventually, even without our taking over the controls, the Universe is so full of Order, it always finds a way to Balance everything, because the Universe cannot exist without perfect Balance. And it will continue to exist.

Second Excerpt:

Everything was miraculous. Everything was so miraculous. Every moment. Every breath that's happening. Every connection we make personally is just the most beautiful, miraculous thing. If we could see what was really going on behind all of this and how much is involved in each one of us and how beautiful it really is -- the bigger picture -- we would really just be in awe all the time. I can see why maybe we need not to be in this state all the time because I couldn't even function. I was going from laughing to crying and things like that. People could have legitimately said "She needs to be locked up" and I would probably have understood...

Learn About Near-Death Experiencer Amy Call
thepurposeoflife-nde.com/contents/

− 30 −

One Of God's Most Astonishing Gifts

Near-Death Experiencer Dr. Mary Neal, M.D.

From the book 7 Lessons from Heaven: How Dying Taught Me to Live a Joy-Filled Life

During the review of my life, Jesus repeatedly allowed me to see both the immediate and distant effects of an event. I was able to appreciate and understand how each event spread through time and space, initiating a cascade of other events from which something of beauty and worth always emerged...

One of God's most astonishing gifts is His ability to use time to heal and redeem: to make something beautiful later out of something that appears ugly now...

Does God really work all things together for our good? During my life review, as I witnessed beauty emerging from every event, my faith in God's promise shifted from a somewhat vague theological hope into complete trust. I understood that He genuinely does make everything beautiful in His time.

7 Lessons From Heaven
thepurposeoflife-nde.com/books/

Learn About Near-Death Experiencer Mary Neal
thepurposeoflife-nde.com/contents/

– 31 –

ALL Experiences Are Essential
IANDS Experiencer #1

I was then led to a room that resembled a conservatory. As soon as I was left alone the walls came to life! 360 degrees of movies, all projected at once. I watched the domino effect of what harsh and unkind words and actions would do to people, how it would start with one person and spiral down to 300 people. I felt the anger and sadness of everyone! I thought I was going to explode! I was emotionally shaken to the core. That was the only semi-negative thing that happened to me during my visit there.

I was asked to return to the library as I was to start my studies, as in reading the scrolls (it was more like downloading into my consciousness). I read and studied there for 60 years!!! Most were people's lives from beginning to end. I was allowed to feel the emotions of most people. Some were vibrant, some were sort of boring. A lot that was downloaded was information. This will be hard to explain, but I'll do my best. We (here on Earth) have a role to play. We choose our lives even before we are born

-- whether we chose a good life or a bad one, it matters not, because there is NO good or bad. It's just your chosen role. And ALL lives lived are essential for our evolution and development. That's why we have memory. WE LEARN AND GROW because we have different lifestyles, beliefs, opinions, etc. Sorry to say this BUT even the most evil -- death, destruction, disease -- is essential! Think about it: if everything was ALWAYS good and going your way; if all relationships were good and everyone got what they wanted, over the years it would get pretty boring and stagnant. I know it sounds wonderful, but it wouldn't let us grow much, would it?

Also, something else that might be hard to comprehend is that there is no such thing as time! Your life is happening all at once, meaning your past/present/future are all one bubble. It's our brain (filter) that makes this so-called time linear. Huh? I know: strange! That might raise questions of free will. Do we have it? Yes and no. Just because your life is predetermined, you don't know what the outcome will be. Things can change on a dime, always remember that! I knew everything about the universe: why, how, what's the point of it all? I was there for so long it was hard not to know everything! When I returned, I couldn't remember a lot of information that I had received. I assumed it was intentional...

Learn About IANDS Experiencer #1
thepurposeoflife-nde.com/contents/

Our Job On Earth Is Important

Near-Death Experiencer Heather V

At the end of this tunnel was the most beautiful place in existence. I seemed to have arrived back in the room but in another dimension. I was looking at everyone and everything in that hospital through what I can only describe as "through the eyes of God." I felt the love of God for all these people in the hospital; the patients, the staff, and the receptionist. I never saw my own life, but I saw everyone else's life pass before my eyes. I saw the receptionist and everything about her. I saw her heart. I felt her love for her babies. I felt her pain and her thoughts. I saw the technician and everything in his life right then. I saw each person for who they really, truly were. I saw what motivated them and I saw their beautiful soul-full hearts. I saw their souls as if through the eyes and heart of God. I saw them and I loved them, each and every person. I seemed to pull back from the room and up, out of the building. I saw people on the street and knew their pain. I saw them with pure love.

Then I began getting an information download. There was no talking, just information going into me with absolute love. It was very clear, very loud, and very certain, that WE ARE ALL VERY IMPORTANT TO GOD. We are all deeply, deeply loved by God and that life is supposed to be hard but that it is some sort of proving ground... The message was that our lives are deeply important to God and to the existence of the universe. Our love we have and the love we cultivate on Earth, especially for people we have a hard time liking, that love somehow expands the universe and does some very important things. I felt that there was something at stake, that we have a very important job to do. Human beings are beloved and our choice in how to act is given to us to prove God. I don't know how to describe it. I am trying hard to explain it here but it's hard to explain. It may take my lifetime to explain what I learned.

Everything seemed to be happening at once; or time stopped or lost all meaning. Absolutely. There didn't seem to be the concept of time in this forever-land. Although it seemed like things moved, which doesn't make sense to Newtonian physics or to Einstein's postulates, this place was a magnificent creation. It was ineffable and reminds me of how does one explain the beauty of Mozart's symphony? But I felt it in its entirety as it was. It seems like when we create beauty on Earth, it is being manifest in Heaven. When we sing on Earth, it is amplified to the golden ratio in Heaven where it becomes like manna, although in this place there is no hunger or thirst. There is just truth and satisfaction.

[I understood] everything about the universe. We are important to God or whatever you want to call It. All religions are trying to explain God but it is just impossible to explain. A true heart which is motivated by loving compassion is what matters in life. Our job is to try to love one another no matter what. It matters very much if we can love or not because that is our job in this world. We must love! This is what we live for and it doesn't mean we must only love our spouse. It means we need to find out how to love our enemy because that is why we are here. We are also deeply important to God. Our job on Earth is important. If we don't learn how to love there are very bad consequences in the multiverse. My sense was strongly that we are needed and our worth is how much we can love.

Yes, I could see the distinction between our life and this other place. The wall between the two worlds is but a filament, thin as a piece of baby's hair. The love we seek is right there resonating right outside us. We need only to call on it. The world here on Earth is not supposed to have all this beauty from the other side. We are supposed to bring the beauty to this world with our love. That is what it needs, human love to bring it into a new consciousness.

In this place we go to, we will have lightness, laughter and joy, and our soul family is there waiting for us. Our jobs on Earth are to find out how to break through all these illusory walls everywhere that we erect to hide who we are. We need to really love each other and love ourselves. I felt as though there was a sense of humor too. I was like a deep appreciation for our lives and even for our failures. We are supposed to learn from our failures and not beat ourselves up over them. We find a way to forgive and love ourselves because in reality, in the real place of creation, there is only love. It seemed the message was that if we couldn't find a path to love, then we are destroying something very, very precious.

My formerly wavering belief in God now is rock solid. It is totally complete without a doubt. That place is the real reality, that place I went to is not this place. This is some kind of proving ground. I know that whomever is reading this, you are deeply loved. Your life is deeply important to God. God is greater than anything you could ever even fathom -- too great for me to even experience. I just felt the presence of God and His love. You, my dear person reading this, are important. Your life is critical. The love you have inside you is beautiful and brilliant and it is needed on this Earth. You can change this world with your love, which is entirely particular to you only. You have your own song.

Learn About Near-Death Experiencer Heather V
thepurposeoflife-nde.com/contents/

- 33 -

Why We Are Here *
Near-Death Experiencer Julie Aubier

When I was 19, I was violently attacked and I had a near-death experience. I completely left my body. First, I saw myself... from the corner of the room... I was looking down at myself... At that moment, I saw my aggressor, I saw what was happening, but I already had no conflict, no judgement about what was happening. I could see the perfection of the situation even though it was a horrible situation.

Then, suddenly, I became the whole frickin universe. I didn't go through a white light. I didn't have beings coming and waiting for me on the other side. I didn't have a voice telling me whatever things I needed to hear. I became the whole universe! I became superconsciousness. I became part of everything and I became everything. I had total clarity and understanding of everything. I could travel and go anywhere I wanted to go. I was extremely free and fearless and eternal. I didn't have a body, but it felt as if I had a body. There was no one with me, but I didn't feel alone. And I felt like I had done this shit so many times.

I was kind of happy to be back there, BUT the thing that was very interesting; the thing that helped me remember why I came on this planet and who I am -- I understood very clearly that coming on the planet was me experiencing a lot of things that I was NOT in order to remember who I was. To understand cold, I had to go through heat, or to understand warmth, I had to go through cold. I understood very clearly as well that being human entitles me to do things that when I am dead, out of my body, I cannot do. Things like drinking a glass of water and this is actually my favorite drink since I came back. I love to drink water. It's always the most mystical experience I've ever had in my life. The pleasure that I have when I'm drinking a glass of water, with my eyes closed, is just out of this world. So drinking a glass of water. Eating my favorite food. Feeling the wind on my skin or the rain on my skin. Swimming naked in the river or in the ocean. Hearing birds singing. Having a beautiful kiss. Making love. Even though there all these different ways of experiencing ecstasy while you are out of your body, the ones that you experience in your flesh are unbelievable. It has to be experienced without attachment, but with pure, total grace, becoming one with the moment, becoming one with the kiss, one with the water, one with the wind, one with the sun, one with birds, one with the people that come in front of you.

I understood as well that I was one with everything; I was the water and I was the mouth that was drinking the water. That every up and down that I experience would teach me something to expand, unless I chose, through free will, to resist what I was going through.

So to me this lifetime is about taking care and cherishing and giving thanks for every little opportunity that I have to experience life in 3D. I know I am eternal; I'm not afraid of death. That's why I am fearless as well. That's why I think and I say what I think. That's why I don't kiss no ass. That's why I don't obey laws and rules that put us in a box and force us to all be the same. I've never been like that. That's why I am one with every mother that cries, every child that is afraid, and every man that gives his life to save another. I am part of all of those people, whatever nation, and country, and status they are. I see the emptiness in most of the people, I see their fear because they don't remember. But if you could only know what I know, you would never take for granted any moment in your life, even the difficult times.

Life is really a school. It's a school to help you remember. A lot of us came as benevolent souls to answer a call. Not necessarily to raise the vibration, but mostly to help others remember who they are; to become the foundation of what is yet to come. Because you see evolution is going to happen with or without us. Humankind is going to get more enlightened and conscious with or without us. We are here because we are the foundation as multi-dimensional beings who live in time-line reality. We can change everything by our presence and desires by what we focus on, what we choose to feed, what we choose to give life to. This is a century where we are going to see women taking their place and being a lot more respected and taken care of.

One thing for sure that I can tell you is that I was an atheist before I had my near-death experience. I still don't follow any religion, but my intuitive skills, my clairvoyance, my ability to see through the bullshit and the lies and the illusion is unbelievable. It has been like this since I came back. Afterwards, I had a few other mystical experiences that confirmed my abilities... It was hard for me originally to understand what happened to me. And I'm a rebel. Even if God came to me and told me, "You are here to save the world," I'm going to say, "Yeah, fuck that; I'm going to go the other way."

Or if He says, "Watch your words and watch your thoughts because everything you say manifests. You are a goddess; you are here to co-create with every word that you use." I would still go and do the exact opposite. But because I have experienced the opposite that I know the power of my attention. I know that each and every time that I focused my attention on something I didn't want, I created it. I created a lot of shit! And I am accountable for that. I want you to remember that.

You are here to live this present moment through the eye of a child; through innocence and purity. Every judgement that you have, every time you close your heart, you hurt a little bit of your soul, but you're going to be alright. Even at the end of it, no one is going to judge you but yourself. You will be accountable for everything you've done here. But not accountable like you are going to be punished. It is not going to happen like that. You are going to be accountable because you will understand and see what you did and what you should have done. And you, from the love of who you are; the immense love that you are, you will want to do something about it and you will not allow it to not be corrected and fixed by yourself...

So love your life. Love every part of it. Understand that you are Divine. You are the whole universe. You are connected to all that is. You are necessary here. The quicker you find peace within and love yourself, the quicker you are going to make this world a beautiful place. And it's going to happen whether you want it or not.

Watch The Companion Video
thepurposeoflife-nde.com/videos/

Learn About Near-Death Experiencer Julie Aubier
thepurposeoflife-nde.com/contents/

Atheists & Skeptics
the-formula.org/how-to-deal-with-skeptics-atheists/

THE PURPOSE OF LIFE

- 34 -

The Sweet Spot

Researcher David Sunfellow

Six centuries ago, a Catholic nun named Julian of Norwich (1342 - 1416), had a near-death experience. Along with discovering, in direct opposition to the church's teaching, that God loved everyone, unconditionally, she also discovered that everything in the universe was unfolding perfectly: "All shall be well, and all shall be well, and all manner of thing shall be well," she declared.

By this she meant that all the injustices we see and experience in this world serve a glorious purpose that lies beyond human comprehension. "Our reasoning powers are so blind now, so humble and so simple," she wrote, "that we cannot know the high, marvelous wisdom, the might and the goodness of God."

If you've read this far, you know many other near-death experiencers report the same thing.

And they go a step further.

Along with declaring that every kind of evil, rotten, distasteful experience under the sun serves the greater good, they also declare that we create our own realities. We aren't innocent victims when our car is stolen, our identity is hijacked, or we (or the ones we love) contract deadly illnesses. Ditto when wars, plagues, political upheavals, economic disasters, fires, floods, earthquakes, and tornadoes turn our lives upside down. On some level, we not only agree to every awful thing that happens to us, but we cheerfully collaborate. Here's how near-death experiencer Natalie Sudman tackled this topic in her book, Application of Impossible Things:

"As outrageous as it may seem to our perspective in the physical, the man who built the bomb that blew me up may have performed that action at my own request. This is not to imply that because it was at my request, his actions are acceptable within the physical world and ought to be overlooked. The role may have been agreed upon in order for the bomber himself to experience what it's like to be chased, arrested, detained, or killed for the violence he visited on others. The bomber's actions don't have to be condoned in the physical world because he and I as Whole Selves agreed to blow me up; we all keep playing our roles within the context of the physical (the collective reality that we as Whole Selves have chosen to focus upon and participate in) according to what we think is good and right.

"That as a Whole Being I actually chose to be blown up flies in the face of more than one cultural base assumption. We generally assume that

things happen to us and that there are many things that we simply can't control. Accidents happen, mistakes are made, some people are lucky, and some are not. My experience simply doesn't support this base assumption. Whether consciously aware of it in the physical mind or not, my Whole Self is fully aware of every experience as a cooperative effort between my focused awareness within the physical world, my Whole Self, and other individual Selves. I craft my physical experiences. Things don't happen to me without my consent; they happen because I created, co-created, or agreed to experience them."

Let's repeat that last sentence:

"Things don't happen to me without my consent; they happen because I created, co-created, or agreed to experience them."

While this is a tough pill to swallow, the blessing in adopting this perspective is that it gives the power back to us. We are no longer victims of outside forces. When we encounter challenging situations, we can turn to the deeper parts of ourselves to find out why. And what to do about them.

Which brings me to the sweet spot.

The sweet spot is first learning, feeling, intuiting that all is well. Then, when we are confronted with aspects of our lives that we are unhappy about, we engage the creative forces within us to find out how we created them, and how they can be changed –

or, if not changed, handled in ways that turn lemons into lemonade.

And speaking of lemonade, let's not forget all the good things in our lives. Near-death experiences also insist that we, in cooperation with the deeper parts of ourselves, create them as well.

Learn About Researcher David Sunfellow
thepurposeoflife-nde.com/contents/

Learn More About Near-Death Experiencer Julian of Norwich
encounters-with-jesus.org/julian-of-norwich/

Application Of Impossible Things
thepurposeoflife-nde.com/books/

Learn More About Near-Death Experiencer Natalie Sudman
thepurposeoflife-nde.com/contents/

- 35 -

I Remembered All The Answers

Near-Death Experiencer Amphianda Baskett

I was very much aware of my earthly life. There was no separation except that in that other "dimension" I was suddenly aware of EVERYTHING -- all the connections, all the "whys" and the answers to the whys of my former life. It's as if all this life I had been in a state of half awareness, or amnesia, wandering around asking "Who I am? Why am I? Why is this so hard? Why why why???" and in that other realm the picture was finally complete. I got all the answers, or I remembered all the answers.

And, yes, there was significant insight into others who I was in relationship with at the time, in particular, my step-mother. I was shown, or could see, her whole life, her struggles, her fears, and all that had made her into who she was. I could finally see her abusiveness was not about me being a "bad" kid. It was ALL because of her fears, her own earthly amnesia, and her struggles, insecurity, etc. I saw that she had been abused growing up. In the end, I could only feel great compassion and even admiration for her (after having seen the truth of her life, her fears, etc.) that she had been through so much pain, and that she bravely chose her life knowing it would be confusing and that happiness would be elusive, but that there were important people she needed to touch, and important experiences she needed to have.

And I saw that it's pretty much exactly the same for ALL human beings on Earth. We are all blind and scared while we are here. We do our best, and it's all understood and our mistakes are forgiven once we have our expanded spiritual awareness back.

Learn About Near-Death Experiencer Amphianda Baskett
thepurposeoflife-nde.com/contents/

— 36 —

No Wonder. No Wonder. No Wonder.

Near-Death Experiencer Barbara Harris Whitfield

Even though I had been an atheist for years, I felt God's love. This love was holding me. It felt incredible. There are no words in the English language, or maybe in this reality, to explain the kind of love God emanates. God was totally accepting of everything we -- God and I -- reviewed in my life.

In every scene of my life review I could feel again what I had felt at various times in my life. And I could feel everything that everyone else had felt as a consequence of my presence and my actions. Some of it felt good and some of it felt awful. All of this translated into knowledge, and I learned. Oh, how I learned!

The information was flowing at an incredible speed that probably would have burned me up if it hadn't been for the extraordinary Energy holding me. The information came in, and then love neutralized my judgments against myself. In other words, throughout every scene I viewed, information flowed through me about my perceptions and feelings, and the perceptions and feelings of every person who had shared those scenes with me. No matter how I judged myself in each interaction, being held by God was the bigger interaction. God interjected love into everything, every feeling, every bit of information about absolutely everything that went on, so that everything was all right. There was no good and no bad. There was only me -- and my loved ones from this life -- trying to survive... just trying to be.

I realize now that without God holding me, I would not have had the strength to experience what I did.

When it started, God and I were merging. We became one, so that I could see through God's eyes and feel through God's heart.

Together, we witnessed how severely I had treated myself because that was the behavior shown and taught to me as a child. I realized that the only big mistake I had made in my thirty-two years of life was that I had never learned to love myself.

God let me into God's experience of all this. I felt God's memories of these scenes through God's eyes. I could sense God's divine intelligence, and it was astonishing. God loves us and wants us to wake up to our real selves, to what is important. I realized that God wants us to know that we only experience real pain if we die without living first. And the way to live is to give love to ourselves and to others. It seems that we are here to learn to give and receive love. But only when we heal enough to be real can we understand and give and receive love the way love was meant to be.

When God holds us in our life reviews and we merge into One, we remember this feeling as being limitless. God is limitless. God's capacity to love is never-ending. God's love for us never changes, no matter how we are. God doesn't judge us either. During our life review, we judge ourselves by feeling the love we have created in other's lives. We also feel the pain we have caused in other's lives. This may be a kind of Cosmic Equalizer. I did not see an old man with a white beard who sits in judgment of us. I only felt limitless divine love.

God only gives. God interjected love into all the scenes of my life to show me God's reality. And the most amazing part of all is that God held nothing back. I understood all that God understood. God let me in. God shared all of God's self with me: all the qualities of gentleness and openness, and all the gifts, including our own empowerment and peace. I never knew that much loving intelligence and freedom could exist.

At this point God and I were merging into one Sacred Person. It felt as though I lifted off the circle bed and We went to the baby I was seeing to my upper left in the darkness. Picture the baby being in a bubble; that bubble was in the center of a cloud of thousands and thousands of bubbles. In each bubble was another scene from my life. As we moved toward the baby, it was as though we were bobbing through the bubbles. At the same time, there was a linear sequence in which we relived thirty-two years of my life. I could hear myself saying, "No wonder, no wonder." I now believe my "no wonders" meant "No wonder you are the way you are now. Look what was done to you when you were a little girl."

My mother had been dependent on prescription drugs, angry and abusive, and my father wasn't home much of the time and did little to intervene. I saw all this again, but I did not see it in little bits and pieces, the way I had remembered it as an adult. I saw and experienced it just as I had lived it at the time it first happened. Not only was I me, I was also my mother, my dad, and my brother. We were all one. Just as I had felt everything my grandmother had felt, I now felt my mother's pain and neglect from her childhood. She wasn't trying to be mean. She didn't know how to be loving or kind. She didn't know how to love. She didn't understand what life is really all about. And she was still angry from her own childhood, angry because they were poor and because her father was sick almost every day until he died when she was eleven. And then she was angry because he had left her. She didn't know what to do with her anger so she gave it to my brother and me. Her anger boiled up all the time and then she physically abused us or she made us listen to all her resentments. Her list went back to her early childhood. Everyone had hurt her. I don't think that she, through her numbness and drugged state, understood how she was doing the same thing to us.

Everything came flooding back, including my father's helplessness and confusion at stopping the insanity. I could hear myself saying, "No wonder, no wonder." And then the benevolent Energy that was holding me held me tighter and with even more love.

We continued watching my mother in pain, always seeing doctors and always receiving prescription painkillers, sleeping pills and tranquilizers. My only feeling during this time was loneliness. I saw myself down on my knees by the side of my bed, praying for a doctor to help my mother. I saw how I had given up "myself" in order to survive. I forgot that I was a child. I became my mother's mother. I suddenly knew that my mother had had the same thing happen to her in her childhood. She took care of her father, and as a child she gave herself up to take care of him. As children, she and I both became anything and everything others needed.

As my life review continued, I also saw my mother's Soul, how painful her life was, how lost she was. And I saw my father and how he put blinders on himself to avoid his grief over my mother's pain and to survive. In my life review, I saw that they were good people caught in helplessness. I saw their beauty, their humanity and their needs that had gone unattended to in their own childhoods. I loved them and understood them. We may have been trapped, but we were still Souls connected in our dance of life by an Energy source that had created us.

This was when I first realized that we do not end at our skin. We are all in this big churning mass of consciousness. We are each a part of this consciousness we call God. And we are not just human. We are Spirit. We were Spirit before we came into this lifetime. We are all struggling Spirits now, trying to get "being human" right. And when we leave here, we will be pure Spirit again.

As my life review continued, I got married and had my own children and saw that I was on the edge of repeating the cycle that I had experienced as a child. I was on prescription drugs. I was in the hospital. I was becoming like my mother. And at the same time, this Loving Energy we call God was holding me and let me into Its experience of all this. I felt God's memories of these scenes through God's eyes, just as I had through my grandmother's eyes.

As my life unfolded, I witnessed how severely I had treated myself because that was the behavior shown and taught to me as a child. I realized that the only big mistake I had made in my life was that I had never learned to love myself.

And then I was back here, in this reality.

AS REVEALED BY NEAR-DEATH EXPERIENCES

Learn About Near-Death Experiencer Barbara Harris Whitfield
thepurposeoflife-nde.com/contents/

Atheists & Skeptics
the-formula.org/how-to-deal-with-skeptics-atheists/

THE PURPOSE OF LIFE

- 37 -

There Is Nothing To Forgive *
Near-Death Experiencer Anita Moorjani

I felt not only that I was loved unconditionally, it was like I just was love just because I existed -- no other reason. I also felt unconditional love for everyone and everything, even for people that may have hurt me during my life. All I felt for them was unconditional love and compassion and a knowing that no matter what they did, even if they hurt me really badly... they were still doing the best they knew how at the time. It was like I understood why they did what they did... that feeling of unconditional love is not even a feeling of forgiveness towards those that hurt you -- it's beyond forgiveness; it's like I understand why you did what you did, and therefore there is nothing to even forgive. Because when I understand you, to me it means you haven't even done anything wrong. To forgive someone means to say you've done something wrong and I forgive you for it. There's a judgement there. There was no judgement... it's almost like having walked a mile in their shoes; it's a knowing that if I was in your shoes, I would have done the same, so there's nothing to forgive. That's the kind of feeling of unconditional love. In that realm this was all I could feel for everyone, and that was what I felt surrounded with. I encountered my father who had passed away 10 years before, and my best friend Soni, who had passed away two years prior to that, and I was also surrounded by other beings who I didn't recognize. But all I felt from them was this unconditional love, as though they were there purely to help me, to guide me, help me through this transition.

Watch The Companion Video
thepurposeoflife-nde.com/videos/

Learn About Near-Death Experiencer Anita Moorjani
thepurposeoflife-nde.com/contents/

- 38 -

Oh Beautiful Human *
Near-Death Experiencer Mellen-Thomas Benedict

First Excerpt:

In 1982 I died from terminal cancer. The condition I had was inoperable, and any kind of chemotherapy they could give me would just have made me more of a vegetable. I was given six to eight months to live. I had been an information freak in the 1970's, and I had become increasingly despondent over the nuclear crisis, the ecology crisis, and so forth. So, since I did not have a spiritual basis, I began to believe that nature had made a mistake, and that we were probably a cancerous organism on the planet. I saw no way that we could get out from all the problems we had created for ourselves and the planet. I perceived all humans as cancer, and that is what I got. That is what killed me. Be careful what your world view is. It can feed back on you, especially if it is a negative world view. I had a seriously negative one. That is what led me into my death. I tried all sorts of alternative healing methods, but nothing helped.

THE PURPOSE OF LIFE

...

There was this Light shining. I turned toward The Light. The Light was very similar to what many other people have described in their near-death experiences. It was so magnificent. It is tangible; you can feel it. It is alluring; you want to go to it like you would want to go to your ideal mother's or father's arms.

As I began to move toward The Light, I knew intuitively that if I went to The Light, I would be dead.

So as I was moving toward The Light I said, "Please wait a minute, just hold on a second here. I want to think about this; I would like to talk to you before I go."

To my surprise, the entire experience halted at that point. You are indeed in control of your near-death experience. You are not on a roller coaster ride. So my request was honored and I had some conversations with The Light. The Light kept changing into different figures, like Jesus, Buddha, Krishna, mandalas, archetypal images and signs.

I asked The Light, "What is going on here? Please, Light, clarify Yourself for me. I really want to know the reality of the situation."

I cannot really say the exact words, because it was sort of telepathy. The Light responded. The information transferred to me was that your beliefs shape the kind of feedback you are getting before The Light. If you were a Buddhist or Catholic or Fundamentalist, you get a feedback loop of your own stuff. You have a chance to look at it and examine it, but most people do not.

As The Light revealed itself to me, I became aware that what I was really seeing was our Higher Self matrix. The only thing I can tell you is that It turned into a matrix, a mandala of human souls, and what I saw was that what we call our Higher Self in each of us is a matrix. It's also a conduit to the Source; each one of us comes directly, as a direct experience from The Source. We all have a Higher Self, or an oversoul part of our being. It revealed Itself to me in its truest energy form. The only way I can really describe it is that the being of the Higher Self is more like a conduit. It did not look like that, but it is a direct connection to The Source that each and every one of us has. We are directly connected to The Source.

So The Light was showing me the Higher Self matrix. And it became very clear to me that all the Higher Selves are connected as one being, all humans are connected as one being, we are actually the same being, different aspects of the same being. It was not committed to one particular religion. So that is what was being fed back to me. And I saw this mandala of human souls. It was the most beautiful thing I have ever seen. I just went into it and, it was just overwhelming. It was like all the love you've ever wanted, and it was the kind of love that cures, heals, regenerates.

...

Then The Light turned into the most beautiful thing that I have ever seen: a mandala of human souls on this planet.

Now I came to this with my negative view of what has happened on the planet. So as I asked The Light to keep clarifying for me, I saw in this magnificent mandala how beautiful we all are in our essence, our core. We are the most beautiful creations. The human soul, the human matrix that we all make together is absolutely fantastic, elegant, exotic, everything. I just cannot say enough about how it changed my opinion of human beings in that instant.

I said, "Oh, God, I did not know how beautiful we are."

At any level, high or low, in whatever shape you are in, you are the most beautiful creation. You are.

I was astonished to find that there was no evil in any soul.

I said, "How can this be?"

The answer was that no soul was inherently evil. The terrible things that happened to people might make them do evil things, but their souls were not evil. What all people seek, what sustains them, is love, The Light told me. What distorts people is a lack of love.

The revelations coming from The Light seemed to go on and on. Then I asked The Light, "Does this mean that humankind will be saved?"

Then, like a trumpet blast with a shower of spiraling lights, The Great Light spoke, saying:

"Remember this and never forget; you save, redeem and heal yourself. You always have. You always will. You were created with the power to do so from before the beginning of the world."

In that instant I realized even more. I realized that WE HAVE ALREADY BEEN SAVED, and we saved ourselves because we were designed to self-correct like the rest of God's universe. This is what the second coming is about.

I thanked The Light of God with all my heart. The best thing I could come up with was these simple words of totally appreciation: "Oh dear God, dear Universe, dear Great Self, I love my life."

THE PURPOSE OF LIFE

...

I had a descent into what you might call hell, and it was very surprising. I did not see Satan or evil. My descent into hell was a descent into each person's customized human misery, ignorance, and darkness of not-knowing. It seemed like a miserable eternity. But each of the millions of souls around me had a little star of light always available. But no one seemed to pay attention to it. They were so consumed with their own grief, trauma and misery. But, after what seemed an eternity, I started calling out to that Light, like a child calling to a parent for help. Then The Light opened up and formed a tunnel that came right to me and insulated me from all that fear and pain. That is what hell really is.

So what we are doing is learning to hold hands, to come together. The doors of hell are open now. We are going to link up, hold hands, and walk out of hell together.

...

One of my questions to The Light was, "What is heaven?"

I was given a tour of all the heavens that have been created: the Nirvanas, the Happy Hunting Grounds, all of them. I went through them. These are thought form creations that we have created. We don't really go to heaven; we are reprocessed. But whatever we created, we leave a part of ourselves there. It is real, but it is not all of the soul.

I saw the Christian heaven. We expect it to be a beautiful place, and you stand in front of the throne, worshipping forever. I tried it. It is boring! This is all we are going to do? It is childlike. I do not mean to offend anyone. Some heavens are very interesting, and some are very boring. I found the ancient ones to be more interesting, like the Native American ones, the Happy Hunting Grounds. The Egyptians have fantastic ones. It goes on and on. There are so many of them. In each of them there is a fractal that is your particular interpretation, unless you are part of the group soul that believes in only the God of a particular religion. Then you are very close, in the same ball park together. But even then, each is a little bit different. That is a part of yourself that you leave there. Death is about life, not about heaven.

I asked God, "What is the best religion on the planet? Which one is right?"

And Godhead said, with great love:

"I don't care."

That was incredible grace. What that meant was that we are the caring beings here.

THE PURPOSE OF LIFE

The Ultimate Godhead of all the stars tells us:

"It does not matter what religion you are."

They come and they go, they change. Buddhism has not been here forever, Catholicism has not been here forever, and they are all about to become more enlightened. More light is coming into all systems now. There is going to be a reformation in spirituality that is going to be just as dramatic as the Protestant Reformation. There will be lots of people fighting about it, one religion against the next, believing that only they are right.

Everyone thinks they own God, the religions and philosophies, especially the religions, because they form big organizations around their philosophy. When Godhead said, "I don't care," I immediately understood that it is for us to care about. It is important, because we are the caring beings. It matters to us and that is where it is important. What you have is the energy equation in spirituality. Ultimate Godhead does not care if you are Protestant, Buddhist, or whatever. It is all a blooming facet of the whole. I wish that all religions would realize it and let each other be. It is not the end of each religion, but we are talking about the same God. Live and let live. Each has a different view. And it all adds up to the Big Picture; it is all important.

I went over to the other side with a lot of fears about toxic waste, nuclear missiles, the population explosion, the rainforest. I came back loving every single problem. I love nuclear waste. I love the mushroom cloud; this is the holiest mandala that we have manifested to date, as an archetype. It, more than any religion or philosophy on Earth, brought us together all of a sudden, to a new level of consciousness. Knowing that maybe we can blow up the planet fifty times, or 500 times, we finally realize that maybe we are all here together now. For a period, they had to keep setting off more bombs to get it in to us. Then we started saying, "We do not need this anymore."

Now we are actually in a safer world than we have ever been in, and it is going to get safer. So I came back loving toxic waste, because it brought us together. These things are so big. As Peter Russell might say, these problems are now "soul size." Do we have soul size answers? YES!

The clearing of the rainforest will slow down, and in fifty years there will be more trees on the planet than in a long time. If you are into ecology, go for it; you are that part of the system that is becoming aware. Go for it with all your might, but do not be depressed. It is part of a larger thing.

Earth is in the process of domesticating itself. It is never again going to be as wild a place as it once was. There will be great wild places, reserves where nature thrives. Gardening and reserves will be the thing in the future. Population increase is getting very close to the optimal range of energy to cause a shift in consciousness. That shift in consciousness will change politics, money, energy.

Second Excerpt:

The next question I asked was "Why would You create humanity? Why would humanity be created when they are such dark and evil beings?"

The Light turned into a mandala, like a big, round stained glass window that was alive and I was breathed into the center of it. In that center, it was like I could look into every human soul, including my own. I could see no evil, at all. No darkness in any human that has ever lived. That may shock you. It shocked me. But I was there in the nexus, the mandala of human souls. There was something in us all -- and in all of nature and all of Gaia -- that's incorruptible, no matter what you've ever done -- it's incorruptible. That is that Source in you that is perfect, that is there already. In that moment, I heard The Light say, "Oh Beautiful Human." It was a blessing. And in that moment, I fell in love with humanity again. I think that's when my cancer was cured.

AS REVEALED BY NEAR-DEATH EXPERIENCES

Watch The Companion Video
thepurposeoflife-nde.com/videos/

Learn About Near-Death Experiencer Mellen-Thomas Benedict
thepurposeoflife-nde.com/contents/

Near-Death Experiences & Miraculous Healings
the-formula.org/miraculous-nde-healings/

THE PURPOSE OF LIFE

We Are Uniquely Special *
Near-Death Experiencer Natalie Sudman

In this non-physical state of being, there is a profound sense of belonging. Everything about everyone that exists is not only accepted, but admired, respected, recognized and celebrated. There is a cooperative, co-passion for being that permeates everything I experienced. Everything there is effortless. It is just so easy. It's blissful. And it's filled with a joy that is so fundamental it's only really remarkable from outside of that state of being. So imagine that everything you have ever thought, imagined, experienced, dreamed, or created was recognized to be valuable to yourself and to everyone else -- to all that exists. Imagine that no matter what you do or how you express yourself, you belong and are valued. This is true. What was known to me, what was so basic as to be assumed was just that: that we are each intrinsically valuable and everything we experience matters, not just to ourselves but to each other and to All That Is.

I use the phrase "All That Is" instead of God, Source, Universe, whatever -- a lot of those words have personal connotations that limit my ideas. And so when I say "All That Is" it includes all that is. That's the term that I'll be using.

My experience is that we are always within and expressions of All That Is which is a beautiful Force of infinitely curious and creative energy and awareness. How can we be anything but perfect? We are All That Is just as much as It is us. We are created by It; It creates us. We participate in It; It participates in us. We extend It and It extends us. We are each individual expressions of this single infinite awareness. We are one. And we are each perfect exactly as we are.

We're so used to thinking in terms of hierarchies. The healer is more important than the addict. The teacher is more important than the arms dealer. These hierarchies of values are not real. I don't care how dull, or weird, or messed up we think our lives are here in the physical world, I can assure you that all of us are having a valuable experience. And I don't care how special we think we are, we are each uniquely special. Every single one of us. Our experience extends and enhances everything that exists. We are each infinitely creative beings having an amazing experience just by being here.

From the out-of-body perspective, it was understood that it takes some skill to even exist in the physical body, in the physical world. It takes a skill of focus to maintain consciousness within a physical body and then to participate in a collective, cooperative, creative experience of being in this physical world. So we're all amazing. We're all jet pilots flying 50 feet off the deck upside down. We are very cool. Just by showing up here, just by showing up.

Watch The Companion Video
thepurposeoflife-nde.com/videos/

Learn About Near-Death Experiencer Natalie Sudman
thepurposeoflife-nde.com/contents/

THE PURPOSE OF LIFE

- 40 -

Dig In, Remember, Teach Others
Near-Death Experiencer Natalie Sudman

We come into this world, at this time, in this place, in order to participate. But that doesn't mean we have to lose sight of the fact of who we really are. We are not this personality, or this body, or these emotions. We are infinite beings having an experience through this body, through the emotions, through the personality.

It is possible to participate in this life, to get into a role with passion while still remembering that it is just a role -- that we are actually whole beings: indestructible, safe, utterly beautiful. The best plays are ones in which the actors are so good, that we all -- actors and audiences -- give ourselves over to the story. But in the end the curtain comes down -- we always know it is a play.

Dig in, be with life, and give yourself over to the story ... without forgetting that it is a story.

THE PURPOSE OF LIFE

...

We're not the only ones who benefit from our experience in the physical world. In this experience, we deepen our understanding of who and what we are in a unique way... When we leave our physical bodies, we have a lot of knowledge that other beings don't necessarily have. We have a lot to teach and share.

Learn About Near-Death Experiencer Natalie Sudman
thepurposeoflife-nde.com/contents/

- 41 -

Everything Was Created For Me
Near-Death Experiencer Jeff Olsen

From the book I Knew Their Hearts: The Amazing True Story of a Journey Beyond the Veil to Learn the Silent Language of the Heart

I saw purpose in every event of my entire life. I saw how every circumstance had been divinely provided for my learning and development. I had the realization that I had actually taken part in creating every experience of my life. I knew I had come to this Earth for only one reason, which was to learn, and that everything that had ever happened to me had been a loving step in that process of my progression. Every person, every circumstance, and every incident was custom created for me. It was as if the entire universe existed for my higher good and development. I felt so loved, so cherished, and so honored. I realized that not only was I embraced by Deity, but also that I myself was Divine, and that we all are. I knew that there are no accidents in this life. That everything happens for a reason. Yet we always get to choose how we will experience what happens to us here... Everything suddenly made sense. Everything had Divine order.

THE PURPOSE OF LIFE

I Knew Their Hearts
thepurposeoflife-nde.com/books/

Learn About Near-Death Experiencer Jeff Olsen
thepurposeoflife-nde.com/contents/

God Has A Plan For Each Of Us

Near-Death Experiencer Dr. Mary Neal, M.D.

From the book 7 Lessons from Heaven: How Dying Taught Me to Live a Joy-Filled Life

If my journey from the bottom of a river to the heights of heaven revealed anything to me, it is that God is not only real and present in our world, but that He knows each one of us by name, loves each one of us as though we were the only person on Earth, and has a plan for each of us that is more significant and rewarding than anything we can dare to imagine on our own.

7 Lessons From Heaven
thepurposeoflife-nde.com/books/

Learn About Near-Death Experiencer Mary Neal
thepurposeoflife-nde.com/content

THE PURPOSE OF LIFE

- 43 -

Anything Is Possible
Near-Death Experiencer Anita Moorjani

The amount of love I felt was overwhelming, and from this perspective, I knew how powerful I am, and saw the amazing possibilities we as humans are capable of achieving during a physical life. I found out that my purpose now would be to live "Heaven on Earth" using this new understanding, and also to share this knowledge with other people. However, I had the choice of whether to come back into life, or go towards death. I was made to understand that it was not my time, but I always had the choice, and if I chose death, I would not be experiencing a lot of the gifts that the rest of my life still held in store. One of the things I wanted to know was that if I chose life, would I have to come back to this sick body, because my body was very, very sick and the organs had stopped functioning. I was then made to understand that if I chose life, my body would heal very quickly. I would see a difference in not months or weeks, but days!

THE PURPOSE OF LIFE

I was shown how illnesses start on an energetic level before they become physical. If I chose to go into life, the cancer would be gone from my energy, and my physical body would catch up very quickly. I then understood that when people have medical treatments for illnesses, it rids the illness only from their body but not from their energy so the illness returns. I realized if I went back, it would be with a very healthy energy. Then the physical body would catch up to the energetic conditions very quickly and permanently. I was given the understanding that this applies to anything, not only illnesses -- physical conditions, psychological conditions, etc. I was "shown" that everything going on in our lives was dependent on this energy around us, created by us. Nothing was solid -- we created our surroundings, our conditions, etc. depending where this "energy" was at. The clarity I received around how we get what we do was phenomenal! It's all about where we are energetically. I was made to feel that I was going to see "proof" of this first hand if I returned back to my body...

I was made to understand that, as tests had been taken for my organ functions (and the results were not out yet), that if I chose life, the results would show that my organs were functioning normally. If I chose death, the results would show organ failure as the cause of death, due to cancer. I was able to change the outcome of the tests by my choice!

I made my choice, and as I started to wake up (in a very confused state, as I could not at that time tell which side of the veil I was on), the doctors came rushing into the room with big smiles on their faces saying to my family "Good news -- we got the results and her organs are functioning -- we can't believe it!! Her body really did seem like it had shut down!"

After that, I began to recover rapidly. The doctors had been waiting for me to become stable before doing a lymph node biopsy to track the type of cancer cells, and they could not even find a lymph node big enough to suggest cancer (upon entering the hospital my body was filled with swollen lymph nodes). They did a bone marrow biopsy, again to find the cancer activity so they could adjust the chemotherapy according to the disease, and there wasn't any in the bone marrow. The doctors were very confused, but put it down to me suddenly responding to the chemo. Because they themselves were unable to understand what was going on, they made me undergo test after test, all of which I passed with flying colors, and clearing every test empowered me even more! I had a full body scan, and because they could not find anything, they made the radiologist repeat it again!!!

Because of my experience, I am now sharing with everyone I know that miracles are possible in your life every day. After what I have seen, I realize that absolutely anything is possible, and that we did not come here to suffer. Life is supposed to be great, and we are very, very loved. The way I look at life has changed dramatically, and I am so glad to have been given a second chance to experience "Heaven on Earth."

THE PURPOSE OF LIFE

Learn About Near-Death Experiencer Anita Moorjani
thepurposeoflife-nde.com/contents/

Near-Death Experiences & Miraculous Healings
the-formula.org/miraculous-nde-healings/

- 44 -

Three Discoveries
IANDS Experiencer #02

I asked a question. All I remember are the answers. A voice boomed so loudly that it could make the universe explode. It said: "Everything is one. There is no past. There is no future. There is only now. And not only that, but every possible outcome, for every possible situation, is occurring at the same time."

The last statement I couldn't quite understand. I was shown an example of being at an intersection behind the wheel of a car and going straight, turning right, turning left, hitting the building on the corner, hitting a light post, going straight up into the air, burrowing into the asphalt -- all at the same time. Every possibility was occurring at the same instant whether I did it or not.

Then I heard, "The largest of the large and the smallest of the small are the same." I became a wave, a spiral, or a tube of sorts that contracted and expanded in and out with the "in" being microscopic and the "out" being infinitely large. I understood to the depths of my being that everything was one and that the smallest atom is the same as the universe. I was turned inside out and became everything, and everything was as tiny as the smallest particle and as huge as the universe. It was all the same, and I was it and it was me.

I was just there, floating in this pure ecstasy, knowing to the depths of my being everything I had just heard and witnessed. Suddenly, I was being downloaded with information about every question I had ever had. I have always been interested in science, physics, biology, human relations, spirituality, religion, etc. In one instant, I understood all there was to know. I particularly remember understanding all about how electricity works, then physics, then human relationships. [I felt] pure joy, and a feeling of simplicity. Then an understanding that it's all love. Everything is love. Everything is one. Everything is now.

Learn About IANDS Experiencer #2
thepurposeoflife-nde.com/contents/

- 45 -

Give Miracles The First Chance
Near-Death Experiencer Mellen-Thomas Benedict

If something ever happened to me again, I would give faith healers and healers the first chance; I would give a miracle the first chance... If someone was all wired up and everything, I would bring a whole bunch of healers in the room, some manifestors, and let them have a go at it. I traveled the world studying these things and I've seen people healed of the most amazing things by holy water, holy places, holy men, holy women, and holy moly. I would give a miracle the first chance... the universe is one giant miracle and you are a part of that!

Learn About Near-Death Experiencer Mellen-Thomas Benedict
thepurposeoflife-nde.com/contents/

Near-Death Experiences & Miraculous Healings
the-formula.org/miraculous-nde-healings/

Aftereffects – Kenneth Ring

Researcher Kenneth Ring, PhD

NDE aftereffects identified by Laurelynn in Kenneth Ring's best-selling book Lessons from The Light

- Increased love for all people and all things

- Increased sensitivity

- Electromagnetic changes

- Increased psychic ability

- Seeing energy -- auras, chakras

- No fear of death

- Lessened fear of many things

- Decreased worry -- surrendering to the divine plan

THE PURPOSE OF LIFE

- Reincarnation beliefs

- Vegetarianism

- Major relationship change -- divorce

- Career change

- Less religious and more spiritual

- Living each day like it is the last

- Living more consciously in the moment

- Increased concern for our planet -- Mother Earth

- Deepened appreciation of nature and the environment

- Knowing that the greatest gift of all is giving love to self and others

- Approaching all humanity and all creation with non-judgment and complete acceptance

- Less materialistic -- seeing the "big picture" of life

- Understanding we have a divine purpose in life

AS REVEALED BY NEAR-DEATH EXPERIENCES

• Understanding the challenges we face are simply lessons to learn here in Earth school

• Knowing with certainty always to follow one's truth and to surrender to the flow of the universe

Lessons From The Light
thepurposeoflife-nde.com/books/

Learn About Researcher Kenneth Ring
thepurposeoflife-nde.com/contents/

THE PURPOSE OF LIFE

Aftereffects – Jeffrey Long

Researcher Dr. Jeffrey Long, M.D.

NDE aftereffects identified by Dr. Jeffrey Long in his best-selling book
Evidence of the Afterlife

- Decreased fear of death

- Increased belief in the afterlife

- A stronger sense of spirituality

- A sense of God's presence

- An awareness of the meaning and purpose of life

- A belief in the sacredness of life

- A greater appreciation of life

- A reduced interest in material gain or status

- Seek out helping or healing professions

- 45 percent report psychic, paranormal, or other special gifts

- People with very serious illnesses, both physical and mental, believe they were healed

- Increasingly loving and accepting of themselves

- More self confidence

- Increased awareness of the needs of others and a willingness to reach out to them

- May end negative and unloving relationships, and seek out positive and loving relationships

- Increasing capacities for love and compassion can result in stronger marriages and relationships

- Increased intelligence (at least in children)

Evidence Of The Afterlife
thepurposeoflife-nde.com/books/

Learn About Researcher Jeffrey Long
thepurposeoflife-nde.com/contents/

- 48 -

Organic Food & Healthy Lifestyles
Researchers Sheila, Dennis, and Matthew Linn

From the book The Gifts of Near-Death Experiences

People who have had NDEs tend to be especially sensitive to their physical environment after they return. They are less able to tolerate anything that is inconsistent with the intensely vital, life-giving energy of the other realm. Thus, they have more adverse reactions to pharmaceuticals, other drugs, and alcohol than previously. Many avoid foods that contain chemicals or artificial sweeteners and prefer organic foods instead. Some become vegetarians. They seek out nature and fresh air. This sensitivity extends to sounds. Many NDEs include music, and NDErs typically feel drawn to music that resonates with their experience. They prefer natural, gentle, melodious sounds and take more pleasure than before in classical or soothing music. They dislike loud, jarring noise.

...

When NDErs return, they tend to gravitate toward whatever is most consistent with physical wholeness, and they usually treat their bodies with greater love and care. For example, they are attracted to alternative medicine, perhaps because it tries to help the body remember its innate wisdom and balance by working with the body's energy systems, rather than by manipulating the body with drugs. Perhaps this shift is a reflection of a change in the energetic frequency of the NDEr, who has returned from an immersion in the highest frequencies of the universe. The person will then be drawn toward what matches that higher frequency. Alternative medicine may be a better match because it emphasizes energetic (or frequency-based) methods of healing… Thus, when NDErs try to avoid chemicals in the form of pharmaceuticals, perhaps they are simply seeking out what best matches them and avoiding what does not.

Similarly, non-organic food has usually been treated with chemicals that are alien to and unrecognizable by the body. These chemicals degrade the food's natural energy, whereas whole organic foods retain more of the energy of life. Since we are made of energy in the form of light, our bodies know the difference. NDErs may be more consciously aware of and sensitive to the energy in substances such as food, since they are likely more aware of the energy in the form of light that constitutes themselves and all things. Thus, NDErs may change their diet. They may also make other changes, such as giving up smoking or drinking, exercising more, and living as close to the Earth as possible.

The Gifts Of Near-Death Experiences
thepurposeoflife-nde.com/books/

Learn About Researchers Sheila, Dennis, And Matthew Linn
thepurposeoflife-nde.com/contents/

THE PURPOSE OF LIFE

Everything Changed

Researcher Kenneth Ring, PhD

From the book Lessons from The Light

According to Neev [a near-death experiencer]... the NDE, and the extended reconsideration of his life it provided, changed everything, bringing about a total reversal of his previous tendencies and even ameliorated long-standing physical problems. The extent of his transformation is remarkable and his summary of it is worth quoting at length.

"I instantly changed from a pessimist to an optimist. There always seemed to be a brighter side to everything. I knew that everything happened for a reason. Sometimes, that reason may not have been clear at first, but in the end, it would all make sense.

"The NDE had a sort of physical healing with me. Physical problems that haunted me all my life disappeared afterward. These problems were chronic migraine headaches, for which I had to take pills for years, cramps, and a terribly anxious stomach, which would act up before school every day, soccer games, tests, and in just about all social situations. Before my experience I was the most klutzy, accident-prone fool you could have ever met. All these problems were solved through my NDE.

"[But] it was not only a physical healer -- my mental state was repaired as well. My outlook on life was no longer bleak and dismal. I felt like I now had a purpose, which was to help people and share my positive perspective. My dependence on time seemed to stop. I no longer felt pressured by the clock -- there was always time to do something else or more. I tried to fit in as much as possible into every day. I experienced everything for what it was -- not for what it could do or give to me. I was no longer interested in what "society" had to say about how I lived my life. I was no longer interested in what people thought or how they felt about me, or if I looked good or not. I learned that I am much more than my body.

"In doing this, other people around me began to accept me for who I was. My feeling of warmth and love flew through from my body and brought me many new friends. I felt comfortable in groups of people to the point that I needed to be surrounded by them. I had no fears of rejection or embarrassment. These were trivial things that had no consequence in the larger scheme of things.

"Pain -- both physical and emotional -- seemed to me to be only a state of mind. Physical pain was a very minor discomfort after my NDE. I realized my mortality, unlike most of my friends. The closeness I had with death kept me from foolishly toying with life, mine and others, like I had before. In learning of my mortality, I also learned to accept death, and in a weird way, I look forward to it. I do not fear many things anymore. Instead, I accept them for what they are and apply them to my life. I tend to try new things more readily, since I want to make the most of my new life without missing a thing.

"From this large change in my personality, many of the things I valued previously seemed virtually unimportant to me. Money and material objects were not even a secondary thought to me. I became very generous with all of my time and material things. I joined several school philanthropy groups and spent time working in several soup kitchens. The most major change I noticed in myself was the loss of the desire to compete. Competition was the major driving force in my life before my NDE, but afterward, it seemed foolish and unimportant. Sports were still fun, but I lost that killer instinct that helped me get recruited by several universities."

From reading this extract, you can see that in essentially every department of Neev's life, he has become the opposite of what he had been before his NDE... By turning Neev inside-out as it were, [Neev's NDE] peeled off his false protective mask and allowed a much more authentic and loving face to show itself to the world. And when it did, the world around him changed accordingly.

And there were other changes, too. Neev found that he had acquired the ability to reenter that otherworldly state during sleep, where he could, in effect, rehearse actions and test their effects before actually performing them in the physical world. Like many other NDErs, he also seemed to develop an extended range of intuitive and psychic perception that sometimes permitted him to know or sense the outcome of events before they took place. Perhaps his greatest gift, however, lay in his enhanced empathic ability. About this, Neev comments:

"These instincts also allow me to empathize with almost anyone. I feel that when I talk to people, I can physically and emotionally feel what they are going through at that time. It is as if I become them for an instant.... The gift of insight allows me to help many people with their problems, but sometimes [it] gets to the point where there are so many that I lose myself in other people."

Lessons From The Light
thepurposeoflife-nde.com/books/

Learn About Researcher Kenneth Ring
thepurposeoflife-nde.com/contents/

Near-Death Experiences & Miraculous Healings
the-formula.org/miraculous-nde-healings/

- 50 -

A Life Greatly Disrupted
Near-Death Experiencer Cami Renfrow

I left my marriage as soon as I could walk again. I experienced ongoing mystical states of consciousness to the point of greatly disrupting my life. I began sensing other people's emotions and physical states. I dropped birth control and influenced my fertility instead through communicating with my unborn children. I experienced major, major neuroendocrine changes, major electrical disruption to the point I had to stop wearing a watch and many holistic medical tests that rely on the electricity of the body do not work on me. Healer after healer in various modalities said they had never seen what they saw was happening in my body (i.e. shaman, clairvoyant, naturopath). I got stopped on the street more than once to be asked what the light was around my head, or from light healers who just wanted to make contact. I dropped western medicine -- despite a shattered pelvis, my children were born at home because they made it clear to me ahead of time that's how it would be safest and healthiest for all of us. My sexuality/libido radically shifted and orgasms began to fill the room around me rather than my body. My family shifted from a middle class normal house to giving our belongings away and living on the road, following intuition rather than society's shoulds.

Learn About Near-Death Experiencer Cami Renfrow
thepurposeoflife-nde.com/contents/

People & Animals Follow Me Home
IANDS Experiencer #3

Forbidden to speak of the encounter, I have kept it to myself all these years although it changed me profoundly. My parents indicated that I became much more compassionate and far less self-centered after this experience. I was able to almost read people's thoughts I became so attuned to others. I still do this.

I also have very unique and close relationships with animals. I have actually been asked to leave the Toronto Zoo because all of the animals I passed came over to stand in front of me in their enclosures. Many pressed themselves right up against the bars or glass and tried to touch me. A woman from another family who was there at the same time as me said that I was "hogging" the animals and their attention to myself, and zoo attendants asked me to wait until no one else was present before I approached the animals. As this happened time after time as soon as I entered a zoo building or exhibit, they eventually asked me to leave even though I was not doing anything but silently appreciating the animals!! Strangers -- particularly children -- still approach me all the time. People and animals have even followed me home for no discernible reason other than to be with me. I have grown used to this behavior and I no longer question it. I also appear to have a VERY green thumb and plants that florists have declared as dead come to life for me. I just seem to know intuitively what to do.

As an adult I was drawn to healing professions and worked for many years in an operating room and other hospital environments. Now I work as an applied anthropologist with adult students whose learning disabilities make post-secondary education difficult. I am frequently told that I have a calming influence on others and that my presence is "soothing".

Since my experience I have also on several occasions been re-visited by animal companions who have passed on, and I now regularly get help from my mother (who has passed on) when I least expect it. I feel as if I am far more open to life/nature and that the boundary between planes of existence is somehow more permeable for me than it was before my encounter. I awoke from my illness (whatever it was) with the certain knowledge that all life is connected, and from that day I have refused to kill anything. I lost my fear of spiders and snakes and I now scoop all insects up and put them somewhere safe when I encounter them.

As an adult I have adopted a Jain philosophy (ahimsa or non-violence) toward life.

Learn About IANDS Experiencer #3
thepurposeoflife-nde.com/contents/

NDEs On The Importance Of Plants, Animals & The Earth
the-formula.org/ndes-on-the-importance-of-caring-for-plants-animals-the-earth/

THE PURPOSE OF LIFE

- 52 -

I Knew Their Story

Near-Death Experiencer Ana Cecilia G

Before the experience, I believed that I was very sensible in most things but I never looked much further than the obvious. After the experience, I knew what was beneath the words of people even without them saying anything. It is as if I knew their story and could decipher perfectly when someone lied to me, or when what they said wasn't real. I was able to read the actions of people as never before. I developed a very sharp sense of perception. It's frustrating sometimes because I can know but I am unable to prove what I know until it happens.

Everything I heard was harmonious, loving with great feeling. I listened to many voices, many sentences, air, water, animals, and it was as if I had the capacity to understand them all. I felt I had brought with me much information but it was so hard to describe. My way of seeing life is very different to how many people see it. I listened a lot and was never confused, the sounds weren't words, but I understood everything. No-one spoke to me, but everyone communicated, I don't know if I have made this clear...

I felt pleasure, immense peace, a love that I have never felt. I felt complete in myself, fulfilled. Everything made sense. I was finally able to unite all the threads of my existence and understand that for which I had been created and why I was here. I felt an immense love for everyone that was here. I adored the animals, and all creation. From that moment on I could never see suffering of an animal or think that the trees and plants didn't have feelings. I felt that everything had a harmonious feeling.

We are all connected, and I felt that there wasn't anything else that wasn't alive in some way. I felt the same towards everyone and everything. Everything was one...

I perceive others clearly. I know when someone is suffering and doesn't show it. I know when someone lies and when someone doesn't tell the truth. I feel much more sensitive towards animals. I can't see them suffer. I love nature and animals. I love people that are near me in spite of whether they have been able to hurt me a lot, I don't feel this bitterness or feed hatred. I gave up focusing on the negative and always try to live more positively.

AS REVEALED BY NEAR-DEATH EXPERIENCES

Learn About Near-Death Experiencer Ana Cecilia G
thepurposeoflife-nde.com/contents/

THE PURPOSE OF LIFE

- 53 -

All The Side Effects
IANDS Experiencer #4

In 1969, when the Apollo astronauts sent back photos of the Earth taken from the moon, I realized what I had experienced was real because I had seen these images ten years beforehand. I never told my parents, and my siblings were told after my parents passed. All the while I felt I had recovered a memory of being in between lives. I never thought I had an NDE until I read an article in one of my nursing magazines two years ago. It listed the physical and psychological side effects of an NDE. I almost fell off my chair as I read. I had almost all of the side effects listed.

For years I've been struggling with being sensitive to loud noise, violence, and bright light. Even the slightest dim light at night bothers me. My normal body temperature is usually 97 or below. I react violently to some medications. And I've had two episodes of anaphylaxis with no discernible cause; the allergist told me I was an enigma. I can't wear a watch for too long because it will run fast, slow down, or just stop working. Right

THE PURPOSE OF LIFE

now I have a dead battery in my watch but as soon as I put it on, it starts to run and will keep running until I take it off. I can't be around electrical things for too long because they will malfunction. Sometimes computers will suddenly drop off line when I walk into the room. In fact this is my third attempt to type all of this and send it to you. The keyboard just seizes up and I can't type.

I have always had some ESP ability. I just "know" when things are going to happen, and I can sometimes "read" minds. I can get just about any plant to grow. And animals love me. One of my friends has a cat, Chubby, who is afraid of people. She runs and hides when company comes over. Yet, when I come over, Chubby runs right over to me wanting to be held. One day, as I sat at my friend's kitchen table drinking tea, the next thing we knew, Chubby was outside at the kitchen window frantically clawing to get in. Once she was let in, she immediately jumped into my lap. My friend never ceases to be amazed.

Even bees and wasps listen to me. If they get in the house, all I have to do is open the door, call them and they fly right out. Now at work, I'm called the bug lady because I can get any bug to go outside. I have had many prophetic dreams. When I was eleven, I dreamed my Dad was going to die two days before he did. I told my sister about the dream but she didn't believe me. She certainly changed her feelings when my Mom got the phone call that dad was dead. After that, for about six months, I was in constant contact with dad. I felt his presence on my right shoulder. All I had to do was think of him and there he was. I could hear his voice in my head and he would answer any questions that I had. My mom found out what I could do and she started begging me to "Ask daddy" all sorts of things. After a while I started to get spooked by all this so I asked my mom not to make me ask dad any more questions.

I always felt the need to nurture. That's why I became a nurse. My patients tell me that I have a very calming presence. Now I am a Reiki Master. Although I don't have a practice yet, I do give Reiki on a consistent basis. Many people comment on my "healing hands." Once I gave Reiki to an autistic girl who lost the ability to speak. I told her I would try to make her feel better. I had my hands on her head for a few minutes when she grabbed my hands and took them off her head. I thought I had probably bothered her, but she put my hands on her face and proceeded to kiss them.

I have often felt that I'm not of this world. It's hard to explain, but I feel out of place. Even though I love life and am so thankful for each and every day, part of me wants to be "back home." I often wonder what would have happened if I could have retrieved more of that memory. It was so frustrating to be so close to going up the stairs then be yelled at and sent back to my body. I have tried numerous times to go back to that memory but I just can't get past that booming voice. Oh well, someday I will.

THE PURPOSE OF LIFE

Learn About IANDS Experiencer #4
thepurposeoflife-nde.com/contents/

- 54 -

Tell Her About The Light
Near-Death Experiencer Louisa Peck

I remembered my near-death experience perfectly, including the bliss of love from The Light I encountered. I missed It terribly. At my core, I knew The Light was real -- but I didn't want to admit it. At the time, even after my NDE, I was an adamant atheist. Anybody who believed in God, or talked about God, just pissed me off. So I discounted my experience. "Get this," I told one friend, "I had this crazy drug trip! It seems like I'm going into the sun!"

In other words, I was really good at denial!

I was raised in a family that dismissed all spirituality as religion – and religion was an archaic way of explaining how the world worked. Now that science had unraveled evolution and biology, it was time to discard primitive beliefs in God, angels, and any related silliness like heaven. My understanding of the universe was simple: it was godless, mechanical, and utterly pointless.

THE PURPOSE OF LIFE

The home I grew up in was also an alcoholic home. In order to survive, I learned to compartmentalize facts I didn't want to integrate into my life. I also became an alcoholic myself.

After my near-death experience, I stood at a crossroads. Either A) everything I had ever believed about a godless universe was wrong or B) I'd had a drug trip. I chose B. That way, I could continue the life I knew of drinking and chasing popularity.

So I locked my NDE away in a vault. I would have left it there except paranormal aftereffects started to happen to me. The greatest one was around my sister's death.

She was dying from metastasized breast cancer. My family and I had been told that she had two weeks to live. During the night, as I tried to sleep in a chair, I sensed light -- The Light -- seeping in the window, traveling to my sister, and swirling in a slow vortex above her body. Each time I opened my eyes, I saw nothing. When I closed my eyes and tried to dismiss the feeling, it grew stronger.

Then a voice, which was connected to the sun I visited in my near-death experience, spoke to me. "She's afraid," It said. "Tell her about The Light!"

"What a silly thought!" I responded. "She's not going to die now. She's gonna live two more weeks!"

"Tell her," the voice urged. Still hesitating, I was shown how my sister's fear and hurt were blocking her from crossing over. I was also shown that I held the key to set her free.

"Go to her!" the voice urged. "Do it NOW!"

At last, I went. I knelt beside her, took her hand, and spoke into her ear. "God loves you so much," I said. Remembering her love for Jesus, I added, "Jesus loves you so much. He's so proud of all you've done on Earth. You've been a wonderful pianist, a scholar, and a loving mother. He's so happy with everything you've done. But your body can't work anymore. It's time for you to come home. Jesus will take you with him. You'll be so warm and the light will fill you with the most amazing love!"

The memory of my near-death experience filled my voice.

"I love you. We all love you."

Twenty minutes later, my sister suffered a violent hemorrhage that sent my brother and I running for help. In a panic, I forgot all about The Light, all about the voice. "Help us! Help us!" Finally, a young doctor came and checked my sister. She briskly informed us, "Her heart is still beating, but it'll stop when it runs out of oxygen." Rage filled me. I wanted to scream, "How can you just let her die?!"

Then, all at once, I could feel my sister's spirit. Her energy was hovering in the room. In life, her love had always felt a certain way, it had a certain flavor. I felt it strongly now. It replaced my anger with joy.

She told me, "I'm fine. I'm so wonderful!" Rejoicing, she filled me, my brother, even the doctor and nurse, with her love. She also filled me with The Light again, which reawakened in me memories of Its brilliance, so much so that I struggled to conceal my joy.

After a series of paranormal events like the one I had with my sister, the last pillar of my atheism toppled. It took 21 years for me to fully align with what I experienced during my near-death experience. In the end, two organizations saved the day: The International Association for Near-Death Studies (IANDS) and Alcoholics Anonymous (AA). These two organizations helped me reach the point where I could tell God that I loved It and promised I would never turn away again -- and I haven't.

My mission, I have come to understand, is to overcome the egoic challenges that all humans face. With humor and humility, we're here to turn fear, anger, selfish greed and gloating pride into love and compassion for all life.

AS REVEALED BY NEAR-DEATH EXPERIENCES

Learn About Near-Death Experiencer Louisa Peck
thepurposeoflife-nde.com/contents/

Atheists & Skeptics
the-formula.org/how-to-deal-with-skeptics-atheists/

THE PURPOSE OF LIFE

- 55 -

I Knew Their Hearts

Near-Death Experiencer Jeff Olsen

From the book I Knew Their Hearts: The Amazing True Story of a Journey Beyond the Veil to Learn the Silent Language of the Heart

I felt the hustle and unrest of the hallway of a hospital. I watched the doctors and nurses as they went about their duties. I moved with ease all around them. I realized none of them were aware of me. They could not see me, but -- wow -- could I see them!

My perceptions were expanded. I knew each person I saw perfectly. I knew their joys and their sorrows. I knew their love, their hate, their pain, and their secrets. I knew everything about them, every detail, every motivation, and every outcome. I knew every emotion they were feeling, and I knew intuitively why they were feeling it. In an instant, with no contemplation, I knew them as well as I knew myself. I knew their hearts...

...I felt spontaneous, intense love for each and every one of them. Not a romantic love, but a perfect, compassionate love...

THE PURPOSE OF LIFE

I moved about the hospital with ease, pausing to take in the beauty of the people I was encountering. I felt their true essence and marveled at the connection I had to each of them, even though I had never met them before...

Most of my life, I had actually avoided people. Now, everyone I saw was truly my brother or sister. In fact it went even deeper than that. THEY were, in a strange sense, ME! We were all connected pieces in a huge puzzle of oneness.

Words Jesus had said rushed to my recollection:

"Inasmuch as ye have done it unto the least of these brethren ye have done it unto me."

Was he talking about the awareness I was experiencing? Did he feel the same thing I was feeling? Was this how he walked the Earth, in the consciousness of knowing each individual soul at this deep level of love?

I realized he didn't see himself as better than the beggar or the prisoner; he knew he was one with them. He knew them perfectly, in the same way I was experiencing the strangers I saw. We are all linked and equal in God's eyes. I was seeing it, feeling it, and experiencing it.

AS REVEALED BY NEAR-DEATH EXPERIENCES

I Knew Their Hearts
thepurposeoflife-nde.com/books/

Learn About Near-Death Experiencer Jeff Olsen
thepurposeoflife-nde.com/contents/

THE PURPOSE OF LIFE

One Day In Manhattan

Near-Death Experiencer Peter Panagore

Every moment of every day God is present to me. I feel less isolated but there are times that I know that my thinking and eccentric behavior makes me the strange one. I like to be out in nature, because out in nature the purity of God's spirit pervades all things -- plants, water, sky, stone, and animals. Out there, I feel most at home.

One day when I was in Manhattan for a few days of work, I went out for a long walk and I prayed. I began to feel the spirit of peace, of contentment and presence that I feel when I walk in the woods and I realized that it was coming from the people around me on the sidewalks. They were nature and radiating the presence of [God] as a tree would, as stone might, as a songbird's song does. I walked for hours through the mass of humanity as if immersed in the wilderness where the spirit of God is strongest.

THE PURPOSE OF LIFE

Learn About Near-Death Experiencer Peter Panagore
thepurposeoflife-nde.com/contents/

Experiencers Will Affect The Entire World

Near-Death Experiencer Mellen-Thomas Benedict

In one of my visits with The Light I was told that the near-death experience... would become more and more popular and it would have an effect on the entire world when a critical mass was hit and all these people have died and come back and are telling you that there is a lot more going on than we think.

Learn About Near-Death Experiencer Mellen-Thomas Benedict
thepurposeoflife-nde.com/contents/

THE PURPOSE OF LIFE

The Next Part Of The Journey *
Near-Death Experiencer Ryan Rampton

I felt like I was not even human anymore, that I had been changed somehow into this spiritual being that walks through life and would look up at the sky and see the trees and feel this amazing, amazing love that God has. It was permeating EVERYTHING. It was in the rocks. It was in the trees and I could feel it. I walked around in this bliss cloud for two weeks just knowing God and feeling His love so profoundly. And then it started to fade and I kind of freaked out and I started to pray: "Heavenly Father, why, why are you pulling away? Am I not being good enough? Is something wrong?"

And He said, "Ryan, I've carried you for two weeks. Now I am walking beside you. You need to learn and reach out and learn how to bring me into you. And how to encourage the relationship we have we each other."

And so that was the next part of my journey...

THE PURPOSE OF LIFE

Watch The Companion Video
thepurposeoflife-nde.com/videos/

Learn About Near-Death Experiencer Ryan Rampton
thepurposeoflife-nde.com/contents/

Only A Memory
Near-Death Experiencer Amphianda Baskett

One of the issues I've had for years and years since is that I get really frustrated that I can't feel God on command in every situation anymore. I don't live in bliss all the time like I did after my NDE. This "failing" of mine has caused me a lot of distress. I couldn't make sense of why I would be given such a vision, such an experience, such a profound awakening, only to lose it, or have it yanked away, leaving me only with a memory of what I used to know and live and feel...

Learn About Near-Death Experiencer Amphianda Baskett
thepurposeoflife-nde.com/contents/

THE PURPOSE OF LIFE

- 60 -

You Can't Keep Any Of The Toys *
Near-Death Experiencer Alon Anava

I felt like trillions of billions of gigabytes of information were being downloaded to me... Imagine a computer; imagine a laptop; a little piece of metal that is worth a hundred dollars. It's nothing. It's a piece of metal. You just take a wire, connect the laptop to the wire. Connect the wire to the wall. And within a split second, this little piece of metal that is worthless has access to all the information in the world using the internet. With one press of a button, any type of search you make on that little piece of metal, that computer, has access to any type of information. I felt like I'm this little entity being connected to the MAIN mother source of information. I can't even say internet. But the MAIN source of information. It's as if an endless amount of information is being downloaded to me simultaneously. This is what it was. I was able to see God's wisdom and derive pleasure. There's no words to describe that pleasure. I get lots of questions like "What did you see? What do you mean you saw God's wisdom? What are the secrets of the universe?" There are really no words to describe it... It's understanding something that is beyond what our mind can understand. Our mind has limits. This is limitless. Something limited cannot understand something limitless.

This whole process -- the downloading of the information -- nothing stayed. I wasn't able, I didn't have the ability to hold it; I didn't have the ability to sustain it. It just washed me. I didn't have the vessel to actually hold that information. As it was going, as pleasurable as it was, there was also a tremendous feeling of the opposite of pleasure that I can't hold it, that I can't sustain it, that I can't grasp it and keep it. It says in many sources that our acts in this world create a spiritual vessel that when our soul leaves the body it has the tool to actually hold that Godly life, to hold that Godly revelation, to be able to hold that Godly wisdom. I wasn't able to hold it. I was able to see it. I was able to enjoy it. But I wasn't able to hold it. So simultaneously it was a tremendous feeling of pleasure and at the same time this very strong feeling of the opposite of pleasure. I really don't know how to define it. It wasn't really sorrow. It was a feeling that I can't keep it. Almost like taking a little kid to a toy store and letting him run there and at the end of it, telling him, "OK, now we have to go home and you can't keep any of the toys. You have to leave all the toys here. Now it's time to go home."

AS REVEALED BY NEAR-DEATH EXPERIENCES

Watch The Companion Video
thepurposeoflife-nde.com/videos/

Learn About Near-Death Experiencer Alon Anava
thepurposeoflife-nde.com/contents/

THE PURPOSE OF LIFE

I Thought I Was Going To Be A Saint

Near-Death Experiencer Howard Storm

After my near-death experience, I wrongly assumed that I was going to be a saint. That I would not have a temper, anger, or lust, or make mistakes at all. That somehow, I had been elevated to this superior person. To my horror, I found out that wasn't the case at all.

...

I was a raging fanatic. I drove my wife and my two teenage children very far away from me by being so obnoxious about their conversion.

THE PURPOSE OF LIFE

Learn About Near-Death Experiencer Howard Storm
thepurposeoflife-nde.com/contents/

Shadow Issues & How To Work On Them
the-formula.org/why-its-important-to-know-about-shadow-issues-and-work-on-them/

Enlightenment Is A Fantasy

Near-Death Experiencer Barbara Harris Whitfield

I've been on this journey for 40 years. I had my NDE in 1975. I see the NDE as the beginning, and this journey is an adventure that never ends. Enlightenment is a fantasy -- as soon as someone announces they are enlightened they "fall" because the label energizes the ego.

Learn About Near-Death Experiencer Barbara Harris Whitfield
thepurposeoflife-nde.com/contents/

Shadow Issues & How To Work On Them
the-formula.org/why-its-important-to-know-about-shadow-issues-and-work-on-them/

THE PURPOSE OF LIFE

Egotism Is A Huge Problem *
Near-Death Experiencer Howard Storm

I want to be a common man. I don't want to pretend to be a saint. My aspiration is to be authentic and I find that to be a real struggle. One of the things that I think is a huge problem with near-death experiencers, and I include myself in that category... is egotism. I've been turned off by some near-death experiencers because I found that their ego was getting in the way of their truth and their authenticity.

Learn About Near-Death Experiencer Howard Storm
thepurposeoflife-nde.com/contents/

Shadow Issues & How To Work On Them
the-formula.org/why-its-important-to-know-about-shadow-issues-and-work-on-them/

THE PURPOSE OF LIFE

A Double Warning
Researcher David Sunfellow

A large number of near-death experiencers report that they felt one of the reasons they had their experience was because they had lost their way in life. Because of this, they required a major wake up call, which is what their near-death experience gave them. A wake up call does not turn formerly dysfunctional people into healthy people. It gives them a story to share, a map to follow, and concrete ways to begin to tackle all the areas of the their lives and personalities that require deepening and healing. What this means is that near-death experiencers, while they often have wonderful stories to tell, including stories of miraculous healings and newfound paranormal abilities, are not necessarily the wisest, healthiest, most evolved people.

So this is a double warning.

First, to near-death experiencers: Spiritual experiences, by themselves, do not transform any of us into perfect beings overnight. We still must do the hard work of purifying egos and integrating spiritual visions and understandings with the practical realities of life. If we try to ride the power of spiritual experiences without doing the hard work of personal transformation, we will end up crashing and burning, and potentially taking a lot of others with us.

Second, to those who are looking to near-death experiencers as emissaries of The Divine: Yes, near-death experiencers have been sent back, in part, to share their stories and, by doing so, help illuminate all of us. Beyond that, near-death experiencers may or may not be able to offer solid, seasoned advice. Along with integrating whatever spiritual experiences they had into daily life, it often takes decades of daily work on shadow and developmental issues to create vessels that allow The Divine to emerge in us in healthy, balanced, full blown ways. The same is true for us. Like near-death experiencers, we must also work on ourselves, which includes not giving our power and personal responsibility away to others who appear to be more evolved than we are.

Shadow Issues & How To Work On Them
the-formula.org/why-its-important-to-know-about-shadow-issues-and-work-on-them/

Experiencers Are Still Human

Researcher Kenneth Ring, PhD

From the book Lessons from The Light

As always, discrimination and discernment must be exercised, because even in "the near-death world"... there are persons, including some NDErs, who are not always what they seem, or who suffer from obvious self-inflation or other grandiose tendencies that any prudent person would do well to eschew immediately... Please remember something that should be obvious: NDErs, though they may have seen The Light, are still human and have human failings. Not they, but only The Light should be exalted. So do not let your enthusiasm for these teachings and for what The Light represents blind you to possible excesses in Its name.

Lessons From The Light
thepurposeoflife-nde.com/books/

Learn About Researcher Kenneth Ring
thepurposeoflife-nde.com/contents/

THE PURPOSE OF LIFE

Don't Pine For A NDE *
Near-Death Experiencer Peter Panagore

If you're pining to have a near-death experience... I would say don't! This is not what you want. It may seem like a blessing, but it is often a curse, as it is a blessing. It leaves one disassociated. It leaves one depressed. I went through a long period of depression. I live a life of non-attachment, not detachment, but non-attachment. My connectivity is to the other side, not so much here.

Watch The Companion Video
thepurposeoflife-nde.com/videos/

Learn About Near-Death Experiencer Peter Panagore
thepurposeoflife-nde.com/contents/

THE PURPOSE OF LIFE

- 67 -

Be Careful What You Wish For *

Near-Death Experiencer Natalie Sudman

I can't tell you how many times I hear "I want the NDE without the ND [near death] part." But there's lots of ways to remember who we are. You don't need to do the ND part.

A lot of people want the flashy spiritually transformative experience of an NDE or something that happens that changes their whole life in an instant. Well, when you have that, unless you have already done the work before you had that experience, you're going to have to do that work after that experience.

What I'm saying is that it may not change your life the way you think it will. It may not change your life that easily. You can start at the beginning and work your way through something and learn it from the bottom up and by the time you get up to that peak experience, it may not feel like a peak because you've worked your way up and it might just fell like "Aaahhhhh, now I'm here." Or you may have that peak experience but then you may crash and have to work your way back up. Or you may find "Oh, I'm losing it" and coming back up and find that road really rocky trying to master what you experienced in an instant.

So what I am saying is a spiritually transformative experience is not always just magic. It can be very disruptive. And very, very difficult afterwards. It may not always be, but it can be. "Be careful what you wish for" is what I am saying. [A flashy spiritual experience] may not be the best way for you. You may be working your way along slowly, slowly, and you may be a lot farther along than you think you are. Just keep going. It's your path. It's your path and your path is valuable for you. Their path is not valuable for you.

Watch The Companion Video
thepurposeoflife-nde.com/videos/

Learn About Near-Death Experiencer Natalie Sudman
thepurposeoflife-nde.com/contents/

Near-Death Experiencers Need To Protect Themselves *

Near-Death Experiencer Tricia Barker

[After my NDE] I was so young, and innocent, and full of love -- this 22 year old young woman -- and I was oblivious to the darkness; I was oblivious to how to protect myself in this world. I think part of my work is to remind young near-death experiencers how to protect themselves. Part of my story is a tough story. I lived in this blissful, happy state of connection with everyone. I loved teaching and I loved my life so much, but when I was in South Korea, I was asleep in my bed and an acquaintance of a friend came in and raped me. I was shocked and horrified. I was this sensitive soul who was completely open to people. I tried to fight in that moment. It was totally shocking. The South Koreans look at foreign women in a different way than they look at South Korean women and all of my Korean female friends said don't even bother going to the police... so I just tried to spread the word as much as I could to other English teachers. Tell them that there are dangers that you might face and to really protect yourselves...

I felt like something was shot right through me and I could see my energetic form and it looked as if I had been shot. It looked like I had this wound that went through me. When I met with other rape victims and rape survivors, I saw that there were different levels of healing that had occurred, as if they were sewing themselves back together. It was beautiful, but it was also very painful because when you saw someone who was just wide open with that wound, then you saw that they had a long way to go; there's a lot of healing to be done. It's a long journey.

I didn't know why I was fated to have that [experience] until years later many of my students -- male and female, even young boys and young girls -- would come to me and tell me their stories of being molested or raped. Sometimes in a crisis situation, I would have to call Child Protective Services and deal with something that was going on in the home at that moment. I was good in those crisis situations because I understood all the things that didn't happen for me. I had to make sure that they were supported, they were loved, they called the police; I had to make sure that everything was done correctly and right for them. I can't tell you how many students I've met over the years from all ages -- from junior high, high school, and college, and at various levels of recovery. They were drawn to me. I was a safe person that they could talk to. So [everything came] full circle. For many years, I was angry and upset. I had to go through the whole healing process, but I realized whatever our wounds are, they prepare us to be stronger and more loving in this world. What I didn't receive, I can now give to others.

Watch The Companion Video
thepurposeoflife-nde.com/videos/

Learn About Near-Death Experiencer Tricia Barker
thepurposeoflife-nde.com/contents/

THE PURPOSE OF LIFE

When Hellfire Preachers Meet A Loving God

Researcher Reverend John W. Price

From the book Revealing Heaven: The Christian Case for Near-Death Experiences

Although they are somewhat simplified labels, "dark" and "happy" may be seen as representing the two ways religious congregations and their leaders go about the process of inserting their perception of God's will into religious practice. The former do so by frightening the faithful with hellfire and eternal damnation, with long lists of dos and don'ts to control unruly human wills. Many people are drawn to this approach, and some churches that proceed in this manner prosper and grow very strong.

I have heard that in some of her lectures Dr. Elisabeth Kübler-Ross related the story of a "hellfire and damnation" preacher who had a heart attack and died, but was resuscitated. As soon as he could, he got back into his pulpit and said, "Everything

I've told you was wrong. God loves us and wants to forgive us. He loves, forgives, redeems." Kübler-Ross did not say what happened next. But, based on several instances I have heard of in which preachers changed their basic message from fear of God to God as love, I might hazard a guess that either the preacher was asked to leave or the congregation dwindled away.

Some preachers build a congregation based on fear of a wrathful, vindictive God who hates sinners. Within American Protestantism this tradition traces its lineage back to Jonathan Edwards during a period of American church history called the "Great Awakening," which occurred between 1730 and 1745. Edwards's 1741 sermon "Sinners in the Hands of an Angry God" epitomizes the Puritan theology of this particular tradition down to this day.

"That was me," wrote Robert, the former fundamentalist pastor I mentioned earlier who had his own near-death experience and was annoyed that he had to return. "In fact, I used to tell people to read 'In the Hands of an Angry God'! I preached mean, angry. I made God out to be a Being to be feared. All that foolishness." During Robert's near-death experience, he left his body and floated away:

"I went into what looked like a womb that was dark, except you could see in the dark. There was a yellow ball that lit up the womb, but even in the dark I could see. P. M. H. Atwater describes this exact scenario in one of her books. The dark place looks like a sonogram of a baby. Yet it's lit by the yellow light, but still was dark. Weird, I know. I believe I went into a womb of some nature to be healed. It was like my hard drive just got completely erased, and I came back to have to relearn."

He rested in this peaceful state for some time -- "it seemed like five minutes" -- and returned:

"The moment I woke up from the coma, I knew that I'd believed a lie that had hurt thousands of people. People would fill the churches up to hear this [lie]. I had a very charismatic personality. It seemed the less I preached in love, the more busy I stayed."

When he returned to his pulpit, he shared his new insight about a loving and forgiving God. The congregation melted away; his income went down to nothing. His family even turned away, except for his loving wife, who liked what he had become. I know of three preachers with similar backgrounds who lost their congregations when they switched to talk about a loving God.

Robert lost his career. He told me, "I can't tell those lies anymore. I can't preach that crap. I hurt thousands of people." He taught a religion of fear and now knows God offers a religion of love. I've had a great and challenging time sharing a loving version of Christianity with him. He is excited about learning to use God's love as a lens to see new insights in scripture. He now says, "Now that I do know the love of God and life, I have no place to share it. In my hospice work, I share my story with all my patients I think are open to it. Never yet had one get offended when I tell them about going into the God of love."

Robert now knows God loves and forgives in every instance when one cries out to him. God gave another chance to the ones with whom I've spoken who were receiving hellish punishment when they cried out, "Lord, help me" or "Jesus, help me." God is not dogmatic or particular to a specific religion or sect. He is universal and, as John tells us, simply love. This revelation led Robert to quit his pastorate.

Revealing Heaven
thepurposeoflife-nde.com/books/

Become The Story
Researcher David Sunfellow

Many NDErs feel compelled to rush out and share their experiences before grounding and integrating them. In my experience, this is usually a bad idea. It's better to ground these experiences in our everyday lives before sharing them with the world. There are several reasons for this. Here are two big ones:

1. It takes time to fully understand what happened and be able to explain it in a way that is truly helpful to others. If we share things too soon, we can promote ideas and practices that are only partially understood. We might return knowing, for example, that the world is a dream. And then create huge problems for ourselves and others by suggesting that everyone and everything we encounter in this world is of no importance; that caring for dream bodies, paying dream bills, and interacting with dream people is a waste of time. Or we may return knowing that everything is perfect just the way it is and create imbalances by refusing to improve ourselves, help

others, address social ills, take care of the planet, or change anything.

2. There is also the danger of creating more instability in our lives and personalities. This can happen as the result of attracting adoring followers who reflect back to us how great we are when we don't have the development to keep our egos in check.

In a similar vein, we can also attract opportunities that can package us into best-selling authors, circuit speakers, and television personalities.

Many people are tempted by this because they think a best-selling book, or an appearance on a popular television show will make everything better. No, that's not the way it works. If we have done the inner work, then we don't need -- and won't be desperately seeking -- the accolades the world offers. If, on the other, we haven't done the work, then we tend to crave outer recognition -- and when it comes, our lives and personalities can become train wrecks. We simply won't have the development necessary to channel all the energy these kind of opportunities pour into our lives and personalities.

When NDErs are sent back and told that part of their purpose is to share their stories with the world, I think they misunderstand this to mean that they are supposed to write a book, become a public speaker, make a movie, be interviewed on talks shows and news programs. It may mean this, but the deeper, truer meaning, may be for them to become embodiments of the love and light they experienced on the other side. The best way to tell their story, in other words, is to become living embodiments of it. If books, movies, and other expressions arise out of them embodying their experiences, they will be able to handle everything in a solid way. If, on the other hand, they seek to manifest these things before they have developed their personalities, dealt with shadow issues, and grounded their experiences in the day-to-day grind of life, then trouble, along with a deep sense of confusion, frustration, and emptiness, are likely to follow.

Learn About Researcher David Sunfellow
thepurposeoflife-nde.com/contents/

Shadow Issues & How To Work On Them
the-formula.org/why-its-important-to-know-about-shadow-issues-and-work-on-them/

THE PURPOSE OF LIFE

- 71 -

Step-By-Step, Little-By-Little
Researcher David Sunfellow

I hear from people all the time who want to have near-death experiences. They want to experience an NDE so they can experience the positive aftereffects that are associated with these experiences. They forget, or may not know, that many negative or challenging aftereffects are also associated with NDEs, not the least of which is learning how to integrate the newfound energies and visions into their day-to-day lives and personalities.

Another fact that is often overlooked is the greater the distance between our earthly personality and the heights we reach during a spiritual experience, the greater the reckoning when we return.

Because of this, my advice is simple: don't waste your time longing for near-death experiences (or any other kind of spiritually transformative experience). Instead, do the daily, challenging, unglamorous work of becoming a better, kinder, healthier, more loving and compassionate person. Step-by-step, little-by-little. And let the spiritual experiences take care of themselves.

This is not to say that there isn't a place for life-changing spiritual experiences. There is. Sometimes we are so lost or stuck that we need to get struck by lightning. That's what is needed to break us free and get us back on track. Or perhaps we need a good shock to help us change course and head off in new directions.

But generally speaking, unless we've built a consciousness that can handle, channel, and ground high voltage spiritual experiences, these experiences will blow fuses all over the place and there will be a lot of cleanup work to do once the smoke clears.

Learn About Researcher David Sunfellow
thepurposeoflife-nde.com/contents/

Shadow Issues & How To Work On Them
the-formula.org/why-its-important-to-know-about-shadow-issues-and-work-on-them/

The Most Frightening Things I Have Encountered

Researcher Dr. Jeffrey Long, M.D.

From the book God and the Afterlife: The Groundbreaking New Evidence for God and Near-Death Experience

The most frightening things that I have encountered in my life were not from fictional books or scary movies, but from near-death experiences with hellish content.

God And The Afterlife
thepurposeoflife-nde.com/books/

Learn About Researcher Jeffrey Long
thepurposeoflife-nde.com/contents/

Hellish & Distressing Near-Death Experiences
the-formula.org/ndes-hell/

THE PURPOSE OF LIFE

As In This World, So In The Next - Only More So

Researcher Kevin Williams

As with heaven, there are various hell realms witnessed by near-death experiencers. We can even see many manifestations of hell right here in the physical realm. There are people in prison, in the Bahamas, in mental institutions, universities, skid row, palaces, crack houses, all kinds of life situations. While hell realms can be seen outside all around the world as a manifestation of an inner hell within humans, hell realms in the spirit world are an even greater manifestation of inner hell within humans. Near-death accounts show that the hell realms in the spirit world are actually the spiritual/mental manifestations of spiritual conditions that humans create within themselves while on Earth.

THE PURPOSE OF LIFE

Learn About Researcher Kevin Williams
thepurposeoflife-nde.com/contents/

Hellish & Distressing Near-Death Experiences
the-formula.org/ndes-hell/

The Beings Of Hell: Common Characteristics

Near-Death Experiencer Samuel Bercholz

From the book A Guided Tour of Hell: A Graphic Memoir

My experience showed me that there are characteristics common to all the beings of hell: they possess a thoroughgoing materialism, combined with nihilism to varying degrees, and attitudes of hatred, disdain, and utter lack of concern or caring for other beings.

A Guided Tour Of Hell
thepurposeoflife-nde.com/books/

Learn About Near-Death Experiencer Samuel Bercholz
thepurposeoflife-nde.com/contents/

Hellish & Distressing Near-Death Experiences
the-formula.org/ndes-hell/

THE PURPOSE OF LIFE

A Spiritual Wakeup Call

Researcher Dr. Barbara R. Rommer, M.D.

From the book Blessing in Disguise: Another Side of the Near Death Experience

The Less-Than-Positive Experience (LTP) is a spiritual wake-up call, causing the person to stop, look back, and review past choices. It can help him or her understand the consequences of those choices, reevaluate thought patterns and "glitches" in thinking or reasoning, and then make necessary changes where indicated. The LTP becomes the nexus point of that individual's path, causing him or her to change their walk and direction.

…

Not only do I believe that it is the person who causes the LTP to happen, but he or she is also responsible for the type of imagery that occurs in the experience and the total content of it. In the LTP, we see what we need to see, hear what we need to hear, and feel what we need to feel in order to do those reevaluations.

THE PURPOSE OF LIFE

Blessing In Disguise
thepurposeoflife-nde.com/books/

Learn About Researcher Barbara R. Rommer
thepurposeoflife-nde.com/contents/

Hellish & Distressing Near-Death Experiences
the-formula.org/ndes-hell/

The Same Level Of Transformation

Researcher Dr. Jeffrey Long. M.D.

From the book God and the Afterlife

Many prior NDE studies used the term "negative" to describe NDEs that were frightening or hellish. I prefer a different label for the hellish NDEs I've studied. Personally, I call them "a walk through the Valley of Death." It is good to remember that most of these are just that, a walk through the valley followed by a new earthly life that may be made more positive by these brief glimpses of that place called hell.

Also of note is the fact that there is historical literary evidence that past saints and holy men and women have experienced descent into hell. And although this brush with evil may be hard on them, it also often provides the grist for a deeper spirituality, one that moves them to greater spiritual wholeness. That is why I prefer not to think of these hellish NDEs as negative. Rather, they are frightening experiences that can lead to the same level of positive transformation as those NDEs that might be described as pleasant.

God And The Afterlife
thepurposeoflife-nde.com/books/

Learn About Researcher Jeffrey Long
thepurposeoflife-nde.com/contents/

Hellish & Distressing Near-Death Experiences
the-formula.org/ndes-hell/

Everyone Can Have A Hellish Experience

Researcher Dr. Barbara R. Rommer, M.D.

From the book Blessing in Disguise: Another Side of the Near Death Experience

It is tempting to think that a "mean" person will necessarily have a frightening or hellish experience, and a gentle, kind person have a blissful experience. Please believe me, that is absolutely not the case. Everyone has the potential of having an LTP (Less-Than-Positive Experience).

Blessing In Disguise
thepurposeoflife-nde.com/books/

Learn About Researcher Barbara R. Rommer
thepurposeoflife-nde.com/contents/

Hellish & Distressing Near-Death Experiences
the-formula.org/ndes-hell/

THE PURPOSE OF LIFE

Sorted By Vibrations
Near-Death Experiencer Arthur Yensen

After death, people gravitate into homogenous groups according to the rate of their soul's vibrations… In the hereafter each person lives in the kind of a heaven or hell that he prepared for himself while on Earth.

If you threw a small pebble into a threshing machine, it would go into the box -- not because it is good or bad, but because of its proper size and weight. It's the same way here. No one sends you anywhere. You are sorted by the high or low vibrations of your soul. Everyone goes where he fits in! High vibrations indicate love and spiritual development, while low vibrations indicate debasement and evil.

When I asked what a person should do while on Earth to make it better for him when he dies, he answered, "All you can do is to develop along the lines of unselfish love. People don't come here because of their good deeds, or because they believe in this or that, but because they fit in and belong. Good deeds are the natural result of being good, and bad deeds are the natural result of being bad. Each carries its own reward and punishment. It's what you are that counts!"

...

[Hell is] a place where everyone retains their physical desires without a way to satisfy them. For example, the glutton can't eat because he has no physical body. The alcoholic can't drink for the same reason, neither can the smoker smoke, nor the drug addict get a fix. The miser can't protect his money, and the sex-maniac, who doesn't believe in love, finds it impossible to satisfy his lust. Hell is a real hell for anyone who lives only to satisfy his selfish desires.

Learn About Near-Death Experiencer Arthur Yensen
thepurposeoflife-nde.com/contents/

Hellish & Distressing Near-Death Experiences
the-formula.org/ndes-hell/

Hell & The Importance Of Kindness

Near-Death Experiencer Samuel Bercholz

From the book A Guided Tour of Hell: A Graphic Memoir

The first-person glimpses of hell... made an unforgettable impact like no other. It's not that I perceived them as a scary warning to change my ways. Rather, the very ordinariness of hell was impressed on me -- the recognition that the hellish inclinations of the ordinary mind are not reserved for exceptionally bad people. Above all, it was a lesson in the importance of kindness -- a lesson almost too simple to seem significant, yet it holds the key to a happy life, and even to liberation itself...

So the bad news is that hell exists -- within our very minds. The good news is that even the worst hell contains the seed of freedom. Hell does not last forever...

THE PURPOSE OF LIFE

A Guided Tour Of Hell
thepurposeoflife-nde.com/books/

Learn About Near-Death Experiencer Samuel Bercholz
thepurposeoflife-nde.com/contents/

Hellish & Distressing Near-Death Experiences
the-formula.org/ndes-hell/

If You End Up In Hell

Researcher David Sunfellow

Near-death experiences make it perfectly clear that God is not sending anyone to hell. We create our own hells -- and heavens -- by the way we live our lives, the thoughts we think, the emotions we express, the way we view and treat ourselves and others.

Many near-death experiencers who report hellish or distressing experiences tend to be excessively materialistic, selfish and self-centered, and/or engage in brazenly self-destructive activities. They also tend to discount, or feel disconnected from, God and other spiritual realities. This includes people who appear to be spiritually motivated, but are really using spiritual and religious trappings to pursue selfish and materialistic goals, such as acquiring money, power and adoring followers. In other words, people who tend to be overly focused on the material world and/or overly disconnected from their spiritual natures, appear to be more likely to experience hellish NDEs.

Hellish and distressing experiences also seem to be related to our overall development, or lack thereof. Since it takes time and experience to grow from immature, self-centered children into mature, conscious, and caring adults, there may be a tendency for young souls to have their lack of development reflected back to them by experiences that are more dense, dark, and dramatic.

Highly developed souls may also have dramatic encounters with hellish realms. These experiences may arise naturally, as momentary events or extended dark night of the soul experiences, wherein souls are purged of impurities by passing -- inwardly and outwardly -- through dark, frightening, and challenging states of consciousness and/or periods in their life.

Whatever determines who has hellish experiences, one thing is perfectly clear: whatever we think, do, and feel in this world is magnified on the other side a hundred/thousand/ten thousandfold, so it's important to develop and purify ourselves as much as we can while we are living on this side of the veil.

What can be done if, for one reason or another, we end up in a hellish realm?

We can remember that we are never alone; The Light, and legions of heavenly helpers, are always present, waiting for us to look up and ask for help.

Along with asking for and receiving help from the Divine, some NDErs also report that hellish experiences are largely fueled by intense emotional reactions. To the degree that we can calm down; take a step back and observe; make a sincere attempt to understand, these experiences not only lose their power, but they reveal themselves to be servants of The Light. If we are brave enough to face and befriend them, they offer us pearls of great price.

Finally, it's important to remember that we are eternal beings made in the image and likeness of our Creator. While it's true that we can scare ourselves (or allow others to scare us), we can't be killed, maimed, broken, tormented, or held captive forever. It is our destiny to remember who we are, what our true nature is, and awaken from all dreams.

Learn About Researcher David Sunfellow
thepurposeoflife-nde.com/contents/

Hellish & Distressing Near-Death Experiences
the-formula.org/ndes-hell/

Shadow Issues & How To Work On Them
the-formula.org/why-its-important-to-know-about-shadow-issues-and-work-on-them/

THE PURPOSE OF LIFE

Cry Out To God
Near-Death Experiencer Howard Storm

To escape the darkness, you must cry out to God. Then the light will appear.

Learn About Near-Death Experiencer Howard Storm
thepurposeoflife-nde.com/contents/

Hellish & Distressing Near-Death Experiences
the-formula.org/ndes-hell/

THE PURPOSE OF LIFE

God, Help Me!

Near-Death Experiencer Cathleen C

I began to hear noise and what I heard was extremely distressing and eventually unbearable. As the noise grew in intensity, I realized it was voices, the countless voices of many, many souls, saying nothing, only weeping and wailing. It was the most anguished, pathetic sound I had ever heard. With every passing moment it grew until I imagined their numbers were in the millions. It was unbearable. I had to get out of this place. But how? I had no body and no voice. Finally, somewhere deep down in my spirit I screamed as hard as I could. I heard my own voice echoing on and on, "GOD, HELP ME!!!" The next thing that happened was a gigantic hand came down and moved under me and lifted me out of that abyss. I was then taken up and up. The anguished voices faded and all was quiet...

THE PURPOSE OF LIFE

Learn About Near-Death Experiencer Cathleen C
thepurposeoflife-nde.com/contents/

Hellish & Distressing Near-Death Experiences
the-formula.org/ndes-hell/

Heaven Is A Frequency
Near-Death Experiencer Teri R

In his presence I felt like I was "Home" in a sense that I have never known before. I saw that my true essence is the energy of love, but as we reviewed my life together, I came to understand how I had removed myself from the benefits and bliss of love through anger. I saw how important it is to project feelings of love because other people can either benefit from or be negatively affected by my energy.

I also came to understand that Heaven isn't a place that you enter but a frequency that you attain. Being in the presence of White Light was "Heaven." It was the greatest feeling I had ever experienced or dreamed was possible. Having that feeling again is what I strive for -- not going to a place. The feeling, the energy I experienced became "The Place."

I understood that you take yourself with you wherever you go. Your own consciousness has to change in order to experience the higher frequencies of love, peace, joy, bliss, and tranquility, which I felt a part of.

So I begged for the opportunity to do just that. I wanted to return because I knew that my consciousness didn't mesh with the unconditional love I was experiencing. I knew that I had to become more loving in order to experience this indescribable love permanently.

Learn About Near-Death Experiencer Teri R
thepurposeoflife-nde.com/contents/

Angels, Angels Everywhere

Near-Death Experiencer Dr. George Ritchie, M.D.

From the book Return from Tomorrow

Gradually I was becoming aware that there was something else on that plain of grappling forms. Almost from the beginning I had sensed it, but for a long time I could not locate it. When I did, it was with a shock that left me stunned. That entire unhappy plain was hovered over by beings seemingly made of light. It was their very size and blinding brightness that had prevented me at first from seeing them.

Now that I had, now that I adjusted my eyes to take them in, I could see that these immense presences were bending over the little creatures on the plain. Perhaps even conversing with them.

Were these bright beings angels? Was the light beside me also an angel? But the thought that had pressed itself so undeniably on my mind in that little hospital room had been:

THE PURPOSE OF LIFE

"You are in the presence of the Son of God."

Could it be that each of these other human wraiths, wretched and unworthy like me, was also in His presence? In a realm where space and time no longer followed any rules I knew, could He be standing with each of them as He was with me?

I did not know. All I clearly saw was that not one of these bickering beings on the plain had been abandoned. They were being attended, watched over, ministered to.

And the equally observable fact was that not one of them knew it. If Jesus or His angels were speaking to them, they certainly did not hear. There was no pause in the stream of rancor coming from their own hearts; their eyes sought only some nearby figure to humiliate. It would have seemed to me impossible not to be aware of what were the hugest and most striking features of that whole landscape, except that I myself had stared at them unseeing.

In fact, now that I had become aware of these bright presences, I realized with bewilderment that I had been seeing them all along, without ever consciously registering the fact, as though Jesus could show me at any moment only so much as I was ready to see.

Angels had crowded the living cities and towns we had visited. They had been present in the streets, the factories, the homes, even in that raucous bar, where nobody had been any more conscious of their existence than I myself had. And suddenly I realized that there was a common denominator to all these scenes so far. It was the failure to see Jesus. Whether it was a physical appetite, an earthly concern, an absorption with self -- whatever got in the way of His Light created the separation into which we stepped at death.

Return From Tomorrow
thepurposeoflife-nde.com/books/

Learn About Near-Death Experiencer George Ritchie
thepurposeoflife-nde.com/contents/

Hellish & Distressing Near-Death Experiences
the-formula.org/ndes-hell/

Angels & Near-Death Experiences
the-formula.org/angels/

THE PURPOSE OF LIFE

A White Glow & Glint Of Lights
Near-Death Experiencer Linda Stewart

A curious manifestation after my near-death experience was that I began seeing a white glow and glint of lights around people and objects. Because I had had so many physical anomalies during my illness, I assumed the "lights" were another, optical side effect of the illness. I was later shown that the lights were far more than that.

As my health had slowly improved, I occasionally drove myself short distances to appointments. One day as I was driving down a busy street, I stopped at a red light and watched an odd scene unfold before me. A delivery truck had parked on the right side of the street about a half-block ahead. The truck was one that opened from the sides rather than the back. I watched as the driver walked around to the traffic side of his truck and began unloading his cargo with oncoming traffic approaching. Inside my car, I said out loud in my little southern voice, "Oh honey, you shouldn't do that, it's dangerous."

THE PURPOSE OF LIFE

On this notable day, I watched, stunned, as the familiar dancing lights around the delivery man swirled, quickly coalescing into the form of a breathtaking, translucent, beautiful woman-spirit, glowing with light.

Perhaps it was because I had sent a loving and concerned thought about the delivery mans' well-being that the spirit turned her loving gaze on me. For a brief moment, our eyes met. She smiled at me, then, hovering over the unsuspecting man, returned her attention to her charge who was oblivious to the heavenly presence and was busily going about his business. I was thunderstruck.

Barely breathing for fear the vision would leave, and mesmerized by the vision, I was reluctant to take my eyes off the beauty of the scene; however, from my peripheral vision, I became aware of even more compelling lights. When I was able to tear myself away from the spirit, I glanced slowly at the vista around me and everywhere I looked, every single person in my view had beautiful, loving spirits attending them. People walking nonchalantly down the sidewalk were accompanied by spirits. From within cars, unfettered by physical barriers, I could see the glow and form of beings around the occupants. I saw joggers with flutters of light streaking behind them as their spirit kept pace. As people entered and left buildings, light beings followed. The view before me was filled with brilliant, white light.

AS REVEALED BY NEAR-DEATH EXPERIENCES

From the limited understanding of my human mind, I struggled to comprehend the meaning of what I saw. I knew the lights were connected to the individual people, although more of them, than with them, almost as if they were an extension of their existence -- a light connection to an aspect of their Higher Self. The lights, a connection to the humans, which were glinting off the beings were so bright and expansive, they interconnected, forming a sort of light grid. I remembered reports in books on the near-death experience of people seeing grids on the other side that they didn't know how to explain.

As I looked at the network of light before me and felt the immense outpouring of love coming from the beings, I realized the connection of human beings to the Beings of Light was through love and that the love itself was connected through this grid.

The metaphor represented by the image I saw and perceived was absolutely clear and I was overwhelmed with the knowledge that WE ARE ALL ONE. I comprehended that our oneness is interconnected by love and is an available, much higher level and means of communication than we normally use but to which we have access. This love is available to anyone who is willing to do the hard spiritual work that will allow us to open our hearts and minds and eyes to Spirit. I remembered the love I had felt in the presence of God and experienced a total sense of love for all existence as an interconnected oneness and a manifestation of God.

Over and over this single truth was being driven home to me. Only God exists, God is everything. All that I gaze upon is a representation of God; not the physical mirage but rather, the shining brilliance behind the mask.

I was startled back to everyday awareness by the blasting of a horn. I looked down at my speedometer and realized I was barely creeping forward in the car. With sheets of tears streaming down my face and all but blind with emotion, I pulled to the side of the road until I could take in all that I had witnessed and regain my composure. I don't know how long I sat, taking in the wonder of that event but I couldn't move until the spectacular vision slowly dissipated, returning to the more familiar form of lights around the bodies of the people I watched...

Learn About Near-Death Experiencer Linda Stewart
thepurposeoflife-nde.com/contents/

Angels & Near-Death Experiences
the-formula.org/angels/

Watch This!

Near-Death Experiencer Tricia Barker

When I was taken in for emergency spinal surgery, I left my body and could see the entire operating room in 360-degree vision. There was a long incision down my spine and hip and the surgery was very bloody. As gruesome as the surgery was, I didn't concentrate on my physical body because I was so pleased that my spirit body existed in a realm beyond the physical. In fact, I was gleeful about this spiritual reality because I had been agnostic before my near-death experience, believing that all consciousness would simply die with the body. Here, in this realm, I knew I had been mistaken. This spiritual reality was more real than any reality I had experienced and certainly more real than a dream.

After rejoicing a moment, I noticed two large, androgynous beings of light. They were eight to nine-feet tall and extremely intelligent. They sent light into my spirit body which calmed me down and let me know how to adjust to this new environment.

THE PURPOSE OF LIFE

This light was energy and information -- a sort of telepathic and energetic communication.

The angels were not only able to interact with my spirit body, but they were also able to interact with the two neurosurgeons and through them. Just before the monitor started to beep, signaling that my heart had stopped, the angels slowed down their communication and looked at me intently. Then, with great force, they said, "Watch this!"

The same light that they beamed into my spirit body, they sent through the back of the doctors, through their hands, and into my physical body. While the surgeons were probably unaware of this interaction, the angels wanted me to know that they could work through them to help pick out the bone fragments from my spine; the angels wanted me to understand that my body would heal, that I would walk again, that they would be helping me energetically, and that I could call on them to aid my healing process. Though I could not process everything the angels were telling me in that moment, I knew that their communication would be something that helped me throughout my life. These messages would wait inside of me for the right time.

My near-death experience continued with a life review, time in a heavenly realm, and an overwhelming moment in the deeply loving presence of God where I would be redirected in my life to work as a teacher. Those first few moments with the angels stayed with me for the twenty-five years that I have worked in classrooms at the junior high, high school, and college level. I often prayed before classes that the angels might work through me to bless the lives of my students. I knew that the angels could work through me to help students just as they worked through my surgeons to help my body heal.

There is a great need for healing and love in this world and if we are willing to be conduits of that love, lives can be transformed. The angels were the point at which my consciousness completely changed. I like to think that many other people's realities have shifted in beautiful ways as they became more aware of their light, their connection to Source, and their ability to heal and create a more positive future for themselves and their loved ones while on their educational journey.

I am grateful every day for the life I returned to after my near-death experience. I am no longer limited in my thinking, but I am connected to a universe of love that wants to be brought into this world in large and small ways. We can all do our part to bring in this love in all of our interactions with others.

Learn About Near-Death Experiencer Tricia Barker
thepurposeoflife-nde.com/contents/

Angels & Near-Death Experiences
the-formula.org/angels/

THE PURPOSE OF LIFE

It's Going To Be OK *
Near-Death Experiencer Cecil Willy

My guardian angel, she was holding my hand, rubbing my arm while I was dying, telling me "It's going to be OK, baby. It's going to be OK." That was the most beautiful human being or entity I have ever seen or witnessed in my entire life. That woman was absolutely flawless. Gorgeous. The most beautiful color skin and hair and eyes. Her touch was so soft and gentle, just soothing. You just knew who she was; that she's always been there. She's still here. And you've got one too! She's standing right beside you, holding your hand. And it's going to be OK.

Watch The Companion Video
thepurposeoflife-nde.com/videos/

Learn About Near-Death Experiencer Cecil Willy
thepurposeoflife-nde.com/contents/

Angels & Near-Death Experiences
the-formula.org/angels/

THE PURPOSE OF LIFE

- 88 -

We All Have Guardian Angels
Near-Death Experiencer Lorna Byrne

We all have a guardian angel. Your guardian angel is there with you now, whether you believe it or not.

I meet lots of people who tell me they don't believe in angels. I do. But then, I have been seeing angels since I was a baby. I see them as physically as I see someone standing in front of me.
I have never seen anyone without a guardian angel. I see them with people of all religions and none, with people who are good and bad, with people who believe in angels and with those who don't. I understand that for some people it's hard to believe that there could be such a thing as an angel, or even that I can see angels. I can't prove the existence of angels, or that I see them. I wish I could. All I can do is tell you what I see and am told and then leave it up to you.

THE PURPOSE OF LIFE

Learn About Near-Death Experiencer Lorna Byrne
thepurposeoflife-nde.com/contents/

Angels & Near-Death Experiences
the-formula.org/angels/

How To Still Storms & Walk On Water

Researcher David Sunfellow

While few in number, some near-death experiencers are shown apocalyptic visions of the future. Earthquakes and tsunamis rage across the Earth. Governments and civilizations collapse. Vast numbers of plants, animals, and people die.

Other near-death experiencers are shown that the worst is behind us. We are now on a path where everything is going to get better and better.

While the specifics and severity of end-of-the-world predictions differ in NDEs, there is one thing they all agree on: a new world is coming; heavenly states of consciousness will eventually manifest in this world.

What can we do to help?

THE PURPOSE OF LIFE

The deepest, most profound near-death experiences tend to be lighthearted and full of hope. There is a playfulness and sense of humor to these NDEs. Instead of raining down fire and brimstone, these NDEs are full of laughter, merriment, and gentle admonitions to lighten up and not take life so seriously.

How can these NDEs be so cheerful when so many apocalyptic possibilities are knocking on our collective door?

One answer is that the higher realms know the world is a dream, no one is really hurt or lost, and everything is unfolding as it should.

Higher states of consciousness also know that everything works out in the end, one way or another.

In other words, the challenges we face in this world are similar to the challenges we face in dreams. After a dream has run its course, we wake up, unscathed. And so do all of our dreaming friends. Even nightmares that are hyper-real and super scary come and go.

Here's the point: whether the world follows a rough path to higher states of consciousness, or a gentle one, we can help by staying connected to the parts of ourselves that know everything is OK.

Instead of getting caught up in the drama of life and injecting more fear, instability, and despair into the collective consciousness of the planet, we can train ourselves to stay calm and connected.

And one more thing.

It's the deep places that produce miracles. And healings. And solutions to complicated and bewitching problems. So staying calm and collected is not simply a way to maintain inner peace, it's also a way to find practical solutions to life's many challenges.

So whatever is happening in your personal life, or in the world at large, I encourage you to go deeper and higher. Engage life, full on, but don't take things too seriously. Be cheerful and light hearted. Joke and laugh. Be a force of nature that not only stops fear in its tracks, but turns the tide and lifts others to higher ground.

This book can help. When negative influences take you hostage and you feel yourself slipping into despair, reach for this little book. It will help you reconnect with the high, calm, healing places within.

THE PURPOSE OF LIFE

Learn About Researcher David Sunfellow
thepurposeoflife-nde.com/contents/

Near-Death Experiences That Predict The End Of The World
the-formula.org/near-death-experiences-that-predict-the-end-of-the-world/

Heavenly Humor In Near-Death Experiences
the-formula.org/heavenly-humor/

- 90 -

The Future Of The World *
Near-Death Experiencer Howard Storm

The world that they showed me in the near future, in a couple hundred years from now, is a world that is difficult for me to understand or accept. What I saw was no visible signs of technology. If there was technology, they hid it from me -- or it was so subtle that I couldn't even see it... I assumed the future would be a world of high technology and they showed me a world of not low technology, but NO technology. Where people's relationship with God, with the creation, and with one another was so intense that human beings controlled the weather of the planet -- not just for the welfare of human beings, but for the welfare of the entire planet. Everybody in the world was telepathically connected to everybody else in the whole world. People raised food by simply meditating or thinking about the food and the food would just grow. They would then pick it and eat it... It was not instantaneous, but it happened before your eyes. Cabbage would grow from a seed to a full grown cabbage in a matter of a few minutes.

THE PURPOSE OF LIFE

People lived in small communities. People could move from community to community, freely, if they wanted to. Most people didn't move around very much. Some communities put an emphasis on music. Some communities put an emphasis on science. Some communities put an emphasis on celebration, liturgy, worship. Some communities spent their time on physical relaxation and enjoyment, sports, and that sort of thing. Some communities were very contemplative and did seemingly very little. Some communities were very active and were very much engaged with their environment, sort of what we would call gardeners, but they were literally environmental sculptors, making these very beautiful places with the vegetation and the geology around them. Different communities had different emphases, but they lived in total harmony with the flora and fauna around them and in complete harmony with one another. The main emphasis of every community was the individuals in the community and most especially the children.

When people had experienced what they felt was their full life experience, there would be a great celebration, and they would lay down and die and their souls, their spirits would be raised up to heaven. Dying was not seen as a sad thing, or grievous thing. It was a joyous time. It was celebrated as a birth.

People ate simply. Dressed simply. From what I was shown, there were no possessions other than the clothes on their back and a few simple instruments like musical instruments, or tools, or things like that which were pretty much shared communally.

It was a world that's very difficult for me to make any sense of because there was great happiness. There was very little suffering. There was no disease because people, with laying on of hands, could heal diseases immediately. The only real suffering that they showed me was sometimes people felt a sense of separateness. And the community would allow these people to feel that, but they would pray for that person, they would surround that person with love and bring that person back into the community. So it was possible for people to move a little bit away from the spirit of the community, but they were brought back into the community. No one was left, no one was ever lost for very long. It was important sometimes for people to feel; to appreciate what they had, they needed to lose a little bit of it once and awhile.

The spirit of Christ lived in every heart -- fully and completely. It's a world that is so unlike the world that we live in. How can we ever get there? But they showed me that this is the world that God envisions for us and it's not that far away.

Watch The Companion Video
thepurposeoflife-nde.com/videos/

Learn About Near-Death Experiencer Howard Storm
thepurposeoflife-nde.com/contents/

THE PURPOSE OF LIFE

Universal Truths (v 2.2)

Researcher David Sunfellow

Based on the core truths presented by near-death experiences from around the world

1. God exists.

2. God is an all-knowing, all-powerful Being who knows and loves everyone.

3. Words cannot describe how profoundly God loves us, or how deeply God is involved in every aspect of our lives.

4. God loves everyone unconditionally; there is nothing we can say, do, or think that can stop God from loving us.

5. While God, the Creator of all life, appears in many forms, He/She/It is most often experienced as a loving, indescribably wonderful Light.

6. God is also experienced as a vast energy field of love and light. Composed of everything in existence, this Divine energy field is alive, sentient, and communicative. So are all the parts that make It up.

7. If we go deep enough, we discover that we are God, The Source of all life. We are also life in all its manifestations.

8. Angelic beings and heavenly realms exist.

9. So, too, do demonic beings and hellish realms.

10. Both are essential and beautiful parts of life.

11. In this world and the next, the realities we experience are created by our thoughts, feelings, and actions.

12. The thoughts, feelings, and actions we focus on in this world are magnified a hundredfold when we cross over to the next.

13. We create our experiences alone and in cooperation with other beings who vibrate at frequencies similar to our own.

14. The more godlike our vibrations, the more godlike the realms and states of consciousness we experience -- and vice versa.

15. Our intentions are more important than what we say and do.

16. God has a delightful sense of humor.

17. So do the angels, guides, and spiritual beings that serve The Light.

18. We should too.

19. We should also lighten up and not take life so seriously.

20. We are immortal, indestructible beings. We should act accordingly.

21. Be brave.

22. Be bold.

23. Follow your heart even if all the world opposes you.

24. The world is a dream.

THE PURPOSE OF LIFE

25. All illnesses, disabilities, and limitations are illusions. Honor their presence and receive their gifts, but don't allow them to define you. You are an eternal being made in the image and likeness of God.

26. When you awaken, all illnesses, disabilities, and limitations will vanish.

27. While the world is a dream, it serves a glorious purpose.

28. If we try to leave this world before we achieve the purposes for which we were born, we get sent back.

29. We are here to love, learn, and have fun.

30. The pursuit of money, fame, and power do not lead to happiness. Ditto for other activities that inflame egos and promote selfish, materialistic goals.

31. Seek to get in your body, not out of it.

32. Honor your body and take care of it. It truly is the temple of God.

33. Honor your intellect and emotions. They are also gifts from God.

34. Seek to fully experience -- and master -- your earthly life.

35. Don't waste your time in this world longing to be somewhere else, including back home in Heaven. You are here because this is where your soul wants to be.

36. Instead of longing to leave this world, bring Heaven here; make the world around you a reflection of higher, more loving, caring, and compassionate states of consciousness.

37. Tackle life's challenges head on.

38. Avoid cheating, short cuts and quick fixes.

39. Remember that you, and everything else, is perfect just the way it is.

(Read 39 again.)

40. Also remember that everything is not perfect and it is your job to make the world (and yourself) better.

(Read 40 again.)

41. When we are one with God, we know everything.

42. When we are human beings, we forget everything, including who we are and why we came here.

43. We remember who we are and why we came here by seeking God and applying what we learn – little-by-little, step-by-step -- to everyday life.

44. Ask God and God's angels, guides, and messengers for their help.

45. The spiritual forces of life have dominion over this world.

46. When we touch, or are touched by, The Divine, miracles of all kinds are possible.

47. Tell the truth – to ourselves and others. Telling the truth connects us with God; dishonesty separates us and creates pain, suffering, and confusion.

48. Admit mistakes.

49. Be humble.

50. Be discerning.

51. Work on shadow issues.

52. Pay attention to dreams. They are connected to everything and reveal, in surprising and magical ways, what we need to know and do.

53. Pay attention to the messages that God sends to us in intuitions, visions, voices, signs, synchronicities, people, animals, nature.

54. Join with others. They see what we cannot see. They are also the main way that God loves us and takes care of us in this world.

55. Get personally involved.

56. Take risks.

57. Be willing to be hurt.

58. When you fall down get back up and try again.

59. Be kind and gentle with yourself. Learn to love yourself as God does.

60. Honor your human weaknesses -- and the human weaknesses of others.

61. Treat others as you want to be treated -- with patience, compassion, and understanding.

62. Be curious and discerning, not judgmental or condemning.

63. Remember when we throw stones, we are throwing stones at ourselves -- literally.

64. Question everything.

65. Don't be satisfied with pat, status quo, superficial answers.

66. Pray (talk to God).

67. Meditate (listen to God).

68. Love and serve others: humans, animals, plants, everything.

69. Remember the little things -- the kind word, the understanding smile, the compassionate touch -- are the big things.

70. Small, heartfelt acts of love change lives and ripple across the universe.

(Read 69 and 70 again. And again.)

71. Give others your full attention.

72. Listen, deeply.

73. Learn and grow.

74. Connect and share.

75. Enjoy life. Have fun.

76. Everything -- every person we encounter, every event we experience, every challenge we face -- has been specifically designed to lift us from lower levels of consciousness to higher ones.

77. Feel and express gratitude for everything, including the challenges in life, which are blessings in disguise.

78. Learn to think intuitively, in non-linear, non-time-based, non-rational ways.

79. Spend quality time in nature.

80. Spend time with others who have experienced The Light.

81. Embrace threshold experiences (birth, death, illness, and other portal-opening events).

82. Study near-death experiences (and related phenomena).

83. While there is evidence everywhere to the contrary, train your mind to look beneath the surface and see the truth: life is good; the world is a beautiful place and you, complete with your human weaknesses and shortcomings, are magnificent.

84. You are known, loved, and cherished.

85. You are unique, essential, and irreplaceable.

86. You have a special role to play in the grand scheme of things.

87. When you find and follow your unique path, which is different from everyone else's, magic happens. You connect with God, you feel happy and fulfilled, all creation rejoices.

88. No matter how many times you try and fail; no matter how far you may be from embodying your full Divine Nature, you will eventually succeed.

89. Don't give up. Don't lose hope.

90. And always remember you are never alone, even when your earthly senses tell you otherwise.

Learn About Researcher David Sunfellow
thepurposeoflife-nde.com/contents/

Learn More About Near-Death Experiences
the-formula.org

AS REVEALED BY NEAR-DEATH EXPERIENCES

THE PURPOSE OF LIFE

Special Thanks
The People Who Made This Book Possible

Many people contributed to this book. Thanks goes first to the experiencers and researchers that are featured here.

I would especially like to thank Kenneth Ring, Barbara Harris Whitfield, Kevin Williams, and Jeffrey Long who cheered me on. Kenneth Ring, in particular, was especially generous with his time, suggestions, and encouragement. Tricia Barker and Louisa Peck also went the extra mile to help me include their stories.

Special thanks to Howard Storm for his fantastic stories, which he graciously allowed me to include in this book. It was his conversation with Jesus that provided the title for the first version of this book and inspired me to wrestle other stories like his into a book (and website) that could be cherished and shared.

I also want to thank all the experiencers and researchers who are not featured in this book, especially the early pioneers who paved the way for the rest of us. Without them blazing new trails, which often included being dismissed, ridiculed, and persecuted by family, friends, co-workers, and authorities of various kinds, this book would never have seen the light of day.

Thanks to my brother Wes, who has not only shared every step of this life with me, but shared every step of my spiritual journey. His love, discerning spirit, and enthusiastic support has been immeasurably important. I also cherish the support of his wife, Shara, my sister in law and spirit.

Thanks to my partner, Alexandra. Along with being one of the most committed, perceptive, and loving people I know, she is also an experiencer. Like so many others, she has struggled to understand and integrate her spiritual experience in this world. I admire, honor, and celebrate both her and her accomplishments. Much of the wisdom contained in this book has been field tested on her -- and vice versa.

Thanks to the small circle of spiritual friends who have been with me for decades, supporting me, challenging me, and cheering me on: Robert Perry, Susan Perry, Ken Froessel, in particular.

Thanks to my sister-in-spirit Maria Cavendish. Maria prodded me, on numerous occasions, to write a book and then gave generously of her time and proofreading skills to help whip this one into shape.

Thanks to my many Sedona friends, especially those who attended my NDE classes and presentations and showered me with praise and appreciation.

Thanks to NHNE's growing NDE communities. Their enthusiastic support, amazing stories, and hard-earned wisdom inspire, teach, and motivate me.

Thanks to my long-time NHNE readers and fans. They've traveled with me from the beginning as I/we sought to answer life's big questions. This book is one of the fruits of my/our labors.

Thanks to God, Jesus, my guardian angel(s), my dreams, and whatever other spiritual forces have been looking after me. Without them guiding, protecting, and keeping a rope tied around my ankles, I wouldn't be here.

Finally, I want to thank my children for loving me and supporting me, even when they weren't quite sure what I was doing or why. To say that I have been obsessed with finding the answers this book contains is an understatement. A significant part of my obsession was a desire to give them (and future generations) what was not available to me: solid, credible answers to life's big questions.

While our ancestors were forced to rely on personal revelations and the spiritual experiences of isolated, often very imperfect

THE PURPOSE OF LIFE

visionaries, the same is no longer true for us. Thanks to the internet, we now have the ability to gather, study, and share the otherworldly explorations of millions of people. This book is a record of the depth, breadth, and power of these ongoing revelations, especially the deeper threads that bind us all together. If the lessons they contain are put to work in our daily lives, Heaven on Earth will no longer be something we dream about. It will become our reality. I look forward to that day -- and to the new adventures that lie beyond it...

References, Links & Resources

All of the source materials used to create this book are documented on the book's companion website. Among other things, the website includes 30 videos and links to the best books, websites, articles, and other materials produced by the experiencers and researchers mentioned in this book.

The Purpose Of Life Website
thepurposeoflife-nde.com

To learn more about near-death experiences, visit these outstanding websites and social networks:

NHNE's Formula Website
the-formula.org

NDE Stories
ndestories.org

Encounters With Jesus
encounters-with-jesus.org

NHNE NDE on BitTube
bit.tube/NHNE

NHNE NDE on Facebook
www.facebook.com/nhnende/

NHNE NDE on Twitter
twitter.com/nhneneardeath

What Near-Death Experiences Teach Us
the-formula.org/resources/what-near-death-experiences-teach-us/

Near-Death Experiences On The Purpose Of Life
the-formula.org/ndes-the-purpose-of-life/

The International Association For Near-Death Studies, Inc. (IANDS)
iands.org

The Near-Death Experience Research Foundation (NDERF)
www.nderf.org

The American Center For The Integration Of Spiritually Transformative Experiences (ACISTE)
aciste.org

Near-Death.com
www.near-death.com

Experiencers & Researchers Featured In This Book

(Numbers indicate chapters)

47 Near-Death Experiencers:

Howard Storm (1, 16, 61, 63, 81, 90)
Tom Sawyer (3)
Reinee Pasarow (5, 7)
Dianne Morrissey (6)
Mohammad Z (8)
Justin U (9)
Oliver John Calvert (10)
Erica McKenzie (11)
Andy Petro (13)
Amy Call (15, 24, 29)
Mary Jo Rapini (17)
Naomi (18)
Anne Horn (20)
Ellyn Dye (21)
Mellen-Thomas Benedict (22, 38, 45, 57)
Ryan Rampton (23, 58)
Jean R (25)
Duane S (26)
Natalie Sudman (27, 34, 39, 40, 67)

THE PURPOSE OF LIFE

Amphianda Baskett (28, 35, 59)
Mary Neal (30, 42)
IANDS Near-Death Experiencer #1 (31)
Heather V (32)
Julie Aubier (33)
Julian of Norwich (34)
Barbara Harris Whitfield (36, 62)
Anita Moorjani (37, 43)
Jeff Olsen (41, 55)
Laurelynn (46)
Neev (49)
Cami Renfrow (50)
IANDS Experiencer #3 (51)
Ana Cecilia (52)
IANDS Experiencer #4 (53)
Louisa Peck (54)
Peter Panagore (56, 66)
Alon Anava (60)
Tricia Barker (68, 86)
Robert (69)
Samuel Bercholz (74, 79)
Arthur Yensen (78)
Cathleen C (82)
Teri R (83)
George Ritchie (84)
Linda Stewart (85)
Cecil Willy (87)
Lorna Byrne (88)

5 Near-Death-Like Experiencers:

Rene Jorgensen (4)
Mary Deioma (12)
John K (14)
Krystal Winzer (19)
IANDS Experiencer #2 (44)

10 Researchers:

David Sunfellow (34, 64, 70, 71, 80, 89)
Kenneth Ring (2, 46, 49, 65)
Laurin Bellg (18)
Jeffrey Long (47, 72, 76)
Sheila, Dennis, and Matthew Linn (48)
John W. Price (69)
Kevin Williams (73)
Barbara R. Rommer (75, 77)

13 Featured Books:

Answers from Heaven (7)
Near Death in the ICU (18)
7 Lessons from Heaven (30, 43)
Application of Impossible Things (34)
Lessons from The Light (46, 49, 65)
Evidence of the Afterlife (47)

THE PURPOSE OF LIFE

The Gifts of Near-Death Experiences (48)
I Knew Their Hearts (42, 55)
God and the Afterlife (72, 76)
A Guided Tour of Hell (74, 79)
Blessing in Disguise (75, 77)
Revealing Heaven (69)
Return from Tomorrow (84)

Notes

Notes

Notes

Notes

Printed in Poland
by Amazon Fulfillment
Poland Sp. z o.o., Wrocław